Jesus never promised us a life without suffering, but he did promise that it is possible to experience peace in all circumstances. In *10 Promises of Jesus: Stories and Scripture Reflections about Suffering and Joy*, Marge Steinhage Fenelon will show you how to live joyfully every day—even in the midst of suffering. Highly recommended!

GARY ZIMAK, *author and radio host*

Boy, do we need this now! Marge Steinhage Fenelon offers us stories of healing and hope, tied to the timeless wisdom of Christ's own words, to lift our hearts and remind us "all things are possible for God." This slender book is a welcome gift for our troubled times—and one that keeps on giving. Take and read. You'll be glad you did.

DEACON GREG KANDRA, *blogger and journalist,*
"The Deacon's Bench" at Patheos.com

Marge Steinhage Fenelon does a masterful job of creating a mosaic of hope by combining the promises of Christ with her own stories and the stories of others in such a way that a beautiful picture of grace emerges. As you read, you will see your own life, your own struggles, and you too will discover how Christ can do marvelous things through weakness.

KELLY WAHLQUIST, *founder of WINE: Women in the New Evangelization, author of* **Created to Relate: God's Design for Peace and Joy**

EWTN Foundress Mother Angelica often reminded her viewers "the cross is not negotiable, sweetheart." In other words, all of us will suffer at some point in our lives and probably more than once. In *10 Promises of Jesus*, Marge beautifully explains, through Scripture and church teaching, how it's what we do with, and what we learn from, life's crosses that can have a profound and very positive affect on our lives.

TERESA TOMEO, *media expert, motivational speaker, best-selling author, syndicated Catholic talk show host of Catholic Connection and The Catholic View for Women*

MARGE STEINHAGE FENELON

10 PROMISES
OF JESUS

Stories *and* Scripture Reflections
about Suffering and Joy

TWENTY-THIRD
PUBLICATIONS
twentythirdpublications.com

TWENTY-THIRD PUBLICATIONS
One Montauk Avenue, Suite 200
New London, CT 06320
(860) 437-3012 or (800) 321-0411
www.twentythirdpublications.com

ISBN: 978-1-62785-281-4
Library of Congress Control Number: 2017959390
Printed in the U.S.A.

 A division of Bayard, Inc.

DEDICATION

For my children, their spouses,

and grandchildren—those now and yet to come.

May you never forget that there's always a reason

and the truth always comes out.

I'm so proud of all of you

and love you all so very much!

CONTENTS

TEN PROMISES OF JESUS

FOREWORD

I've taught my children countless practical lessons, some of which they still remember and a few I'm sure they'd prefer to forget. But there are two lessons that I expect they not only remember but also will repeat to their own children one day.

There's always a reason.
The truth always comes out.

They've heard me repeat these two axioms so often that I've heard them murmur them to themselves before I've even had a chance to speak. Not only do they know what I'm about to say, but they know that it's true.

I don't remember when I first started using these two sentences, but looking back now, it seems like I knew them from the time I was a small child. God's providence is never random, and there is a specific reason for everything he does and allows, even when we remain completely puzzled. In our limited human intelligence, we can't possibly know all that God knows. In fact, there are some things that we shouldn't

1

know and that must be left to his wisdom alone. Because of our human failings, we're prone to dishonesty, imprudence, doubt, and discouragement. We also can be clueless at times about what's going on. In those circumstances, there is a truth; it's just that we don't know what it is. God does, though, and the truth must always be revealed even if it takes until the end of the world.

There's always, always a reason, and the truth always, always comes out. God will make certain of that. But we must trust him to do so and allow him to do it in his own way and in his own time because he knows what is best for us.

This is true also when we're experiencing sorrow. We may not know the reason for it, and we may not know the truth about it, but God does. No matter the cause, there's a reason for our sorrow, and the truth of it will come out even if it takes a very long time. And, when all is said and done, we'll find that our sorrow has been turned to joy. That's our Lord's promise to us.

It's my conviction of this that prompted me to write this book. I want you to see that, no matter how terrible your sorrow is right now, one day—maybe sooner, maybe later—your sorrow will be turned to joy. The ten promises outlined in this book are ones made by Jesus and in his own words. They're not assumptions of what he might have meant or summaries of things that he said. They're his words, expressed with purpose, knowledge, wisdom, and the power of God. The examples used in each of the chapters are real-life situations of people who were brave enough and kind enough to share their stories with me so that others might also trust in our Lord's promises. Because of the sensitive nature of the various situations, some of the people who shared their stories requested that I use fictitious names and hide other identifying factors. I did so, gladly, to protect their privacy. But be assured that, even if the names are not real, the way their sorrow was turned joy is completely real. With permission, I used the real names of the others so that readers may benefit from the ministries that have come to life because of their sorrows. Whether the names are real or not, what is real is the way Jesus fulfilled his promises to them.

I pray that you can see a part of yourself in the examples I've used and the people who shared them. It's often by considering someone else's crosses that we gain courage and strength to carry our own. The stories of others can help us to have hope that our own stories will end in joy as well.

May our Lord Jesus Christ bless you with faith and trust in his merciful love, no matter what sorrows you may endure. May he send his Spirit upon you to light your way.

MARGE STEINHAGE FENELON
Pentecost 2018

TRUST *the* PROMISES: JESUS IS *the* TRUTH

Jesus said to him, "I am the way and the truth and the life. No one comes to the Father except through me." JOHN 14:6

J esus did not say I *tell* the truth, although he most certainly did. He did not say I *know* the truth, although he undoubtedly did because he is God. No, Jesus said I *am* the Truth.

It's notable that all other great religious leaders—Buddha, Confucius, Plato, and Mohammed, for example—left behind a written code for their followers. Jesus, on the other hand, left the world without leaving any written message whatsoever. The truths that other ethical teachers proclaimed were not *in* them, but rather *outside* them. Our Lord, however, identified Wisdom and Truth with himself. That was the first time in all of history that it had ever been done, and it has never been done since.

Jesus is indeed Son of God and the Word Incarnate. He is the Way, Truth, and the Life. Without the Way, there is no direction. Without the Truth, there is no knowledge. Without the Life, there is no living. Jesus told his disciples that, except through him, there would be no possibility of salvation. He is the only one in all of history who has made himself the condition of securing eternal life.

In his acclaimed book *Life of Christ*, Venerable Fulton J. Sheen wrote,

> There is no such thing as seeking first the truth and then finding Christ, any more than there is any point in lighting

tapers to find the sun. As scientific truths put us in an intelligent relation with the cosmos, as his stark truth puts us
in temporal relation with the rise and fall of civilizations,
so does Christ put us in intelligent relation with God the
Father; for he is the only possible Word by which God can
address himself to a world of sinners.[1]

Jesus isn't the source of light; he is the Light itself.

And so, when he says, "I am the Truth," he isn't really referring to the words that he chooses to speak. Rather, he's referring to everything he thinks, does, says, and is. What's more
is that Jesus not only identified himself with all Truth and
Life, but also with judgment. He told his followers that, as the
Judge, he would return again, seated on a throne of glory and
attended by the angels to judge all men and women according to their works. No mere man could or would ever be able
to penetrate the depths of all consciences, discern all hidden
motives, and pass judgment on them for all eternity.

In his divinity, he asks us to love him above all else, even to
the point of courageously facing persecution, enduring trials
of all kinds, and sacrificing our own bodies to save our souls
and be united with him in eternity. At the same time, Jesus
tells us that he is meek and humble of heart. What human
being could possibly make such a claim?

Sheen wrote,

When one takes into account his reiterated assertions about
his divinity—such as asking us to love him above parents, to

---

1 *Life of Christ*, by Fulton J. Sheen, ©1958, McGraw-Hill, p. 156.

believe in him even in the face of persecution, to be ready to sacrifice our bodies in order to save our souls in union with him—to call him just a good man ignores the facts. No man is good unless he is humble; and humility is a recognition of truth concerning oneself. A man who thinks he is greater than he actually is is not humble, but a vain and boastful fool. How can any man claim prerogatives over conscience, and over history, and over society in the world, and still claim he is meek and humble of heart? But if he is God as well as man, his language falls into place and everything that he says is intelligible. But if he is not what he claims to be, then some of his most precious sayings are nothing but bombastic outbursts of self-adulation that breathe rather the spirit of Lucifer than the spirit of a good man.[2]

Since Jesus, then, is Truth itself, what he preached in the Sermon on the Mount must in fact be absolutely true. On that mount, he spoke the Beatitudes—eight statements of blessedness that have since become known as the "essence of Christianity."

THE BEATITUDES

Blessed are the poor in spirit, for theirs is the kingdom of heaven.

Blessed are they who mourn, for they will be comforted.

Blessed are the meek, for they will inherit the land.

Blessed are they who hunger and thirst for righteousness, for they will be satisfied.

---

2   Ibid, p. 160.

Blessed are the merciful, for they will be shown mercy.

Blessed are the clean of heart, for they will see God.

Blessed are the peacemakers, for they will be called children of God.

Blessed are they who are persecuted for the sake of righteousness, for theirs is the kingdom of heaven.

Blessed are you when they insult you and persecute you and utter every kind of evil against you [falsely] because of me. Rejoice and be glad, for your reward will be great in heaven. Thus, they persecuted the prophets who were before you. ✳ *Matthew 5:3–12*

Jesus preached the Sermon on the Mount after spending forty days fasting and praying in the desert (during which he was tempted by Satan), after having called his first disciples, and at the beginning of his ministry in Galilee. Before each major step in his mission, our Lord spent time in solitude and prayer. This is also the case during his time in the desert. So, when he chose his disciples, his choices were carefully made and after serious contemplation. When he delved into his ministry in Galilee, one of the first things he did was to teach the Beatitudes. The sermon was not comprised of off-the-cuff remarks given to placate the gathering crowd. Not at all. They were given as a directive for all lives and as a foreshadowing of Christ's own life on earth. The Beatitudes aren't a take-it-or-leave-it suggestion; they are mandates for all Christians.

However, these mandates carry with them our Lord's solemn promises that we will be indeed blessed by following them. The poor will become rich; those who mourn will be comforted. The meek will inherit the land; those who crave righteousness will find satisfaction; the merciful will be given mercy; the clean of heart will see God; peacemakers will be given their rightful place as God's children; those who are persecuted will inherit the kingdom. In all, what Jesus is saying in the Beatitudes is that our sorrow—whatever kind of sorrow it is or however long it lasts—will be turned to joy.

Remember that the Person who said that, who indeed promised that, is no braggart of a man. No, the One who spoke the Beatitudes, who promised that our sorrow would be turned to joy, is Jesus Christ himself. And Jesus Christ is the Way, the Truth, and the Life. Notice that there is no clause in the Beatitudes that says their promises will be fulfilled only in certain circumstances. Their promises will be fulfilled in *all* circumstances, for all time. Jesus is God, the Almighty, All-powerful, All-knowing, All-wise, and All-loving God. It's not possible for him to tease, exaggerate, mislead, or lie. He speaks not only as the One, but also as the One who has himself experienced our human suffering. There is no degree of anguish that we are asked to suffer that he has not already suffered for our sakes. That is the meaning of the cross. It's also the meaning of the resurrection.

St. Teresa of Ávila (1515–1582) lived during a time of political, social, and religious upheaval. Called to Christ, she entered the Carmelite Order despite strong opposition from her father. But, much to her sorrow, she saw that a spirit of worldliness had encroached upon her community, and they were no longer living the ideals of their founder. She had professed her vows with great love for the Carmelite spirituality and, I'm sure, hopes for a grace-filled and spiritually abundant life among her fellow nuns. I imagine she must have felt as though all of her joy had turned to sorrow when she realized that the order she'd entered was no longer the order to which she belonged.

A great mystic, she was a woman of prayer, discipline, and compassion—her heart belonged to God alone. In her times of prayer, she sought God's consolation and enlightenment to know what to do with her sorrowful situation. The answer came that she should found a new convent of Carmelites, one that would truly live the order's rule of life. Eventually, what St. Teresa of Ávila began became the Discalced Carmelite order.

St. Teresa wrote a series of letters to the sisters in her convent, directing them in the Carmelite ways and encouraging them toward holiness and fervency. These letters later were published in book form as *The Way of Perfection*.

In one of her letters, the saint shared wisdom about clinging to God even when being given a heavy cross to bear.

But even this consideration is a poor remedy, and not a very perfect one. It is better that your cross should continue, that you should fall into disgrace, and be despised: desire this may be so, for the sake of that Lord who is with you. Cast your eyes on yourselves, and behold yourselves interiorly, as I have said already: there you will find your Master, who will not be wanting to you, and the less *exterior* consolation you have, so much the more will He caress you. He is very compassionate, and never fails to help the afflicted and disconsolate, if they trust in Him alone. So saith David, "Mercy shall encompass him that hopeth in the Lord." Either you believe these words, or you do not: if you *do*, why do you torment yourselves? O my Lord! did we truly know Thee, we should not be anxious for anything, for Thou givest plenty to those who wish to trust in Thee. Believe me, friends, if we understand this truth, it will be of great assistance towards enabling us to discover that all the favors of this world are a *lie*, even should they hinder the soul but a little from retiring into herself. Would that you could understand this truth. I cannot make you understand it; for though I am obliged, more than any one else, to understand it, yet I cannot understand it as I ought to do.[3]

St. Teresa admitted that even she didn't fully understand all that there was to know about God's truth. Yet, she believed with all her heart that our Lord never will abandon those who suffer if only they trust in him. The heavier our burden, the more consolation we will receive from divine love, according to his promise.

---

3 *The Way of Perfection and Conceptions of Divine Love*, by Saint Teresa of Ávila, trans. Rev. John Dalton, C. Dolman, ©1852.

TEN
PROMISES
of JESUS

SEEK FIRST HIS KINGDOM

"Therefore I tell you, do not worry about your life, what you will eat [or drink], or about your body, what you will wear. Is not life more than food and the body more than clothing? Look at the birds in the sky; they do not sow or reap, they gather nothing into barns, yet your heavenly Father feeds them. Are not you more important than they? Can any of you by worrying add a single moment to your life span? Why are you anxious about clothes? Learn from the way the wild flowers grow. They do not work or spin. But I tell you that not even Solomon in all his splendor was clothed like one of them. If God so clothes the grass of the field, which grows today and is thrown into the oven tomorrow, will he not much more provide for you, O you of

little faith? So do not worry and say, 'What are we to eat?' or 'What are we to drink?' or 'What are we to wear?' All these things the pagans seek. Your heavenly Father knows that you need them all. But seek first the kingdom [of God] and his righteousness, and all these things will be given you besides. Do not worry about tomorrow; tomorrow will take care of itself. Sufficient for a day is its own evil." MATTHEW 6:25–34

How many times have you heard or read that Scripture passage? If you're like me, you've heard it more times than you can count. Every time I hear it, it gives me comfort.

Yes, yes, God will take care of me. Everything will be just fine.

It's such a beautiful image—almost romantic, in a way—of birds and flowers and wild grasses that grow and flourish under God's providential care. When I meditate on it, I'm immediately transported in my mind to the beautiful prairie lands of the United States during the days of the great westward expansion. Free, flowing, full of life and color, the lands speak loudly of God's tender care without uttering a single word. When I go to that special Scripture-place, I feel as though I haven't a single care in the world. It makes sense to me that, if God takes such good care of birds, lilies, and field grass, how much better will he take care of me? I'm secure in God's divine providence.

But then, when I'm in the thick of things and when life seems to be going badly for me or someone I love, it's easy to forget all about this wonderful passage. Faced with adversity, I'm no longer among the wildlife and flora of the prairie and am instead trapped in the quagmire of my personal concerns. I go back to worrying and to doubting God's providence in my life. I don't mean to doubt God, of course, but I do because I can't help myself. The vision of this Scripture passage and the reality of my present situation seem to be two completely different things—incompatible and irreconcilable.

It seems matter of course that God will take care of the things of nature because they are his creation. But what about me? What about the things that are going on in my life right here, right now? Certainly, I can trust nature to God, but can I trust myself to God? Can I trust to his care the people and situations that concern me?

Jesus assures us that we are more precious to him than the birds, or the flowers, or the grass in the field. He tells us not to worry about what we'll eat or drink or about what to wear. In this passage, our Lord names these things specifically, but he is using food, water, and clothing as inclusive of all the various cares we have in our lives. He doesn't want us to worry; he wants us to trust him. He cautions us against anxiety, which can be harmful to our well-being both spiritually and physically.

Spiritually speaking, anxiety becomes an obstacle to our deepening relationship with God. Imagine your own human relationships and the effect anxiety can have on them. How deep can your relationship with another person be without trust? How can you feel secure in your love when you're worried about the other's ability to come through for you when you need them? If you're spending your time fretting rather than growing closer, there can't be much of a relationship between you. It's the same with your relationship with God. If you spend your time fretting about what will happen to you if you don't allow yourself to completely trust God, you'll have far less energy to focus on getting to know him as the loving Father that he is for you. You simply can't place yourself into the hands of Someone you don't trust, and you can't fully trust when anxiety is holding you back.

There's more. When Jesus warns us against anxiety, he's not only referring to the effects it will have on our souls; he's referring to the effects it will have on our bodies as well. His question, "And which of you by being anxious can add one cubit to his span of life?" isn't a metaphor; it's a factual statement. According to research conducted by Harvard Medical School, anxiety can take its toll on your health and even can shorten your lifespan.

> Anxiety has been implicated in several chronic physical illnesses, including heart disease, chronic respiratory disorders, and gastrointestinal conditions. When people with these disorders have untreated anxiety, the disease itself is more difficult to treat, their physical symptoms often become worse, and in some cases they die sooner.[4]

Worry, fretting, and anxiety will do us no good. In fact, they will cause problems for us. That's why our Lord wants us to live in the here and now and to trust in him to provide all that we need. Those who cannot do this Jesus calls "men of little faith." Today is what counts, Jesus says; tomorrow will have worries enough of its own.

Mother Angelica called this living in *The Present Moment*. "The word worry means 'to live in,'" she said. "He doesn't want you to live in the future. Only God knows what your future will be—or even if you will have a future. Jesus has pleaded

---

4   Harvard Health Publications, Harvard Medical School, "Anxiety and Physical Illness", June 6, 2017, http://www.health.harvard.edu/staying-healthy/anxiety_and_physical_illness, accessed July 27, 2017.

with us and shown us his example. He wants us to live in this Present Moment. Do it. Now."[5]

This kind of worry-free living requires us to always be centered on Christ and to seek above all else his kingdom and his righteousness. If we do that, Jesus promises, all that we need will be given to us.

Elise[6] wrote to me one day, telling her story of how Jesus had fulfilled this promise in her life. It's a story of unexpected trauma, struggle, and living in the here and now. I was instantly attracted to it because it so perfectly exemplified Jesus' promise that, if we seek first his kingdom, all that we truly need will be ours.

ELISE: HE IS REAL

Elise grew up in a traditional Catholic family in the Chicago suburbs. In her junior year of high school, she met Dan,[7] her future husband. They married when Elise was twenty-two, and Dan found work as a television news consultant. God blessed them with three children—two girls and one boy. Although Elise loved her husband and children dearly, she did not love the fact that Dan's career caused them to move six times in eight years. She was a self-described "homebody," and the moves made her feel as though God was playing a joke on her.

---

5 *Mother Angelica's Little Book of Life Lessons and Everyday Spirituality*, ed. Raymond Arroyo, ©2007, Doubleday, p. 26.

6 Not her real name.

7 Not his real name.

In time, Dan became dissatisfied with what he perceived as a lack of ethics in his industry, and so he made a career change, and the family relocated to Texas. Within a year, Dan lost his job and was diagnosed with stomach cancer. More than one thousand miles from family and friends, Dan and Elise were forced to form a new support network that, thankfully, resulted in lasting friendships. Dan succumbed to the cancer and died soon thereafter.

"I tell everyone that [God] gave us everything we could have asked for except for Dan to get well," she wrote to me.

Additionally, her two then-grown children moved to Texas to help their parents and have remained close to Elise since.

Left to fend for herself on a preschool teacher's income and one child yet at home, Elise was faced with a serious financial situation. Even in this dark hour, God's light shone through. She was able to sell her house, secure a job as a kindergarten teacher, and rent an apartment across the street from the school. Although lonely and missing the presence of a spouse, she was discovering the grace of God in her circumstances— being alone was allowing her a freedom she'd never experienced before. She was learning to like her independence.

So, when a fellow teacher suggested she meet her son's single father-in-law, she made it clear that she wasn't interested in a committed relationship. That changed the instant she met Andy,[8] who was smart, funny, and good looking. The connection was immediate, and by their second date, they knew there was something serious between them. They soon became engaged and then married, becoming a blended

---

8   Not his real name.

family with five children ages thirty-six to twenty-one. Elise and Andy were happy together in a way that was very different from the happiness that she'd shared with Dan.

Then one day, tragedy struck. Without warning, Andy was diagnosed with a systemic staph infection that resulted in eighteen days in intensive care, several major surgeries, a heart stent, two more months of hospitalization, rehabilitation, and a series of ups and downs.

Elise was plunged into a faith crisis. "In the blink of an eye, everything had been turned upside down," she wrote. "All the joy was gone and there was fear everywhere! If I got to keep him, what would that look like? Would he be a quadriplegic? How would I care for him? What quality of life would he have? Would I love him? What about our finances? There was a crisis practically every day, and it was two steps forward, three steps back over and over."

When Dan had been sick, Elise had felt God there beside her. Not this time. This time she felt completely empty and spiritually dry. She fell apart, wrestling with God over what appeared to be a cruel joke. Why did he give her a gift just to take it back and leave her in despair? Despite being on her knees day after day in the hospital chapel, God didn't seem to be answering her prayers—at least not in the way she wanted him to. During prayer one day, Elise was reminded of Mother Teresa's dark night of the soul and how the saint had kept praying through it. She resolved not to give up, either. Her prayers led her to imagine the Blessed Mother and the women of Jerusalem during the carrying of the cross, and she realized that she was experiencing the same agony of watching a loved one being tortured without being able to do anything about it. She felt as though she actually was walking the way of the cross with our Lord.

Additionally, Elise had to handle Andy's home-based engineering firm without any business background or engineering knowledge. Not knowing who else to turn to, she contacted Kristen,[9] the woman who had designed Andy's website. Kristen knew nothing about engineering, either, but she did know that Elise needed help, and so she flew from her Illinois home and moved in with Elise, and together the two of them somehow managed to keep the business afloat. They became best friends. In Kristen, Elise found a stronghold of support and encouragement who not only helped her in the business but also helped her out of her faith crisis.

After two months, Andy showed signs of recovery and was allowed to go home. He needed a wheelchair and still required a great deal of medical care that had to be administered by Elise around the clock. Despite the difficulties and uncertainties, Elise felt God's guiding hand.

"It's taken a whole year and our life is still only about 90% back to normal," she wrote. "God was asking a lot of me. It's not my nature, but the only way that I could have peace was to listen to Kristen, find my buried faith, and give it all back to him. I had no choice but to slow down, put my trust in him, and allow him to work through the doctors, therapists, and Andy at his pace even though it would mean months and months of challenges."

Elise found her way to acceptance through journaling and keeping a family calendar, on which she marked each step of

9   Not her real name.

Andy's progress. She resumed her weekly Adoration hour too. As the weeks passed, Elise could see the miracles unfolding, and she knew she was coming out of the desert of her spiritual crisis. When she felt the dryness creeping back into her soul, she'd look back on the journal and calendar pages to remind herself of how far they'd come.

As Andy continued to improve, one question persistently nagged Elise. *Why had Andy received a miracle and not Dan?* The only plausible explanation was that she and Andy—two ordinary people—were called to share the joy of the miracle they'd received with others. Elise believes that she's been called to spread the good word.

She ended her story with this: "Goodness knows this very sick world needs hope. God is real. He is here with us. He is still working miracles. He loves me, and I love him and am so grateful. This year has been the hardest of my life, but I've been given so much. God is good, and we are blessed."

Elise's struggle of faith is a source of encouragement for all of us. In a very real way, she had to force herself to become like the birds, flowers, and grasses in the Scripture passage— totally dependent on God and trusting in his care. Day by day, she allowed herself to be tended to and led by our Lord, not just once, but many times over, even though it was against her nature. Yet she did it because she had faith in God, and her faith became the pathway of trust for her. Elise was able to keep before her what mattered most—to seek first his kingdom and righteousness.

When everything seems to be going wrong, the last thing you might want to do is to stop trying to make it right and depend on God to take care of your problems. Perhaps Elise's story can help you to see that God is real and loves you deeply. To grapple with your faith in difficult times is no shame, as long as you continue, through the struggle, to seek first his kingdom and righteousness.

HE WHO COMES TO ME SHALL NOT HUNGER

Jesus said to them, "Amen, amen, I say to you, it was not Moses who gave the bread from heaven; my Father gives you the true bread from heaven. For the bread of God is that which comes down from heaven and gives life to the world." So they said to him, "Sir, give us this bread always." Jesus said to them, "I am the bread of life; whoever comes to me will never hunger, and whoever believes in me will never thirst." JOHN 6:32–35

I *am the bread of life.* Jesus got into trouble by saying that. He spoke those words during what is known as The Bread of Life Discourse, when a crowd had gathered around him after the miracle of the loaves and fishes. They wanted to be fed again, but our Lord explained that the *real* food they needed did not come from the land or sea but rather from heaven. They pushed him for an explanation, and so he gave it to them. He told them point blank that *he* was the Bread from heaven that was given for their salvation:

> "Amen, amen, I say to you, unless you eat the flesh of the Son of Man and drink his blood, you do not have life within you. Whoever eats my flesh and drinks my blood has eternal life, and I will raise him on the last day. For my flesh is true food, and my blood is true drink. Whoever eats my flesh and drinks my blood remains in me and I in him. Just as the living Father sent me and I have life because of the Father, so also the one who feeds on me will have life because of me." ✳ *John 6:53–57*

These are radical words. They were far too much for his disciples to accept, and so "many [of] his disciples returned to their former way of life and no longer accompanied him" (John 6:66). Even today, these words are hard to accept for many. And so, like the confused and unbelieving disciples, they return to their former way of life and no longer accompany our Lord. Sometimes, it's even we ourselves who walk away in disbelief.

Believing in Jesus means believing in his word. His words are true, direct, and without compromise. When Jesus says something, he means it. So when he says that he is the Bread of Life, he knows exactly what he's talking about and is purposeful in saying it. He doesn't want us to sorrow, whether by our own actions or by the actions of others. Instead, he wants us to have life in its fullest sense of the word.

You might say that Abigail[10] learned this lesson the hard way. She suffered at the hands of a neglectful mother, alcoholic father, and sexually abusive brother. For a time, she turned away from God, uninterested in a Being who could allow such terrible things to happen. Still, our Lord was faithful in his promise and eventually drew Abigail back to himself. In his great love for her, Jesus wanted to satisfy Abigail's hunger with the Bread of Life.

ABIGAIL: RETURN TO THE SACRAMENTS

Abigail's father was a functional alcoholic, and her mother was mentally and emotionally detached from reality. She had two siblings—an older brother and a younger sister. The children seldom saw their father, because he worked evenings. Her memories include him working until very late, coming home drunk, and being extremely angry if she came out of her bedroom to greet him. Several times she was beaten with a belt or yardstick.

On Abigail's wedding night, her mother revealed the awful truth that she never should have married her father. In fact, she had intended to break up with him the night he proposed,

---

10 Not her real name.

but she saw him as a way to escape her own miserable life with a functional alcoholic father. She thought that she might learn to love him. Abigail's parents' marriage was a tumultuous one, with many extramarital affairs and long periods of time when the children were left home alone or with an ill-equipped babysitter. One babysitter had even locked the children in the basement while she had a huge party upstairs.

The lack of security caused Abigail to be uncontrollably fearful, particularly of thunderstorms—a fear that worsened when, at age ten, her family home was struck by lightning. That was the only time Abigail's family had prayed the rosary together. Other than that, she has no memory of discussing faith during her childhood, but she does vaguely remember having a children's prayer stool when she was small and using it to say night prayers. The family attended church at Christmas and Easter, and the children were sent to religious education classes. Still, she has no memory of ever having been in church together as a family.

Her memories of even being at home are scant as well. She often was sent to her maternal grandparents' house on weekends and whenever she was ill. She has faded memories of being sick and uncomfortable and sleeping on someone else's bed or on their couch. Her grandfather would become angry when she was there, especially when she was ill. Then her grandparents would argue in Portuguese—their native tongue—making Abigail feel even worse. Eventually, her grandparents divorced, and she blamed herself for it.

Although Abigail's father was well-liked and had many friends who visited often, he had a terrible temper that he often let loose on the family. He had a heart attack when he was in his early thirties that scared him and gave him pause. For the first time, Abigail's father told her, "I love you," and she was sure that her world was about to change. Sadly, within a year, things went back to the way they were. Abigail began to withdraw from her father. When she turned twelve, he had another heart attack. She decided to visit him in the hospital and when she did, he shouted at her for taking so long to visit and for being an "ungrateful, spoiled kid." Unfortunately, the change in her father had been only temporary.

Abigail's mother was an incredibly needy person whose compliments were backhanded putdowns. She was a sad and broken person, and Abigail took it personally. Abigail became angry at God for sending her a mother who was a source of pain and anguish and not a source of unconditional love as she should have been. She'd cry herself to sleep at night hoping her mother would come to comfort her, but her mother never came. Instead, she'd scream at Abigail to be quiet because she was bothering her. Her mother spent hours, sometimes days, in bed, not rising to care for her family, and yelling at the children from her bedroom. The real cause of her behavior was severe depression, but Abigail was convinced it was because she was a terrible person that not even a mother could love. Consequently, the children were starved for affection and left to their own devices.

Abigail believes now that this is what led her brother to sexually abuse her, beginning when she was very little. She was four years younger than he; he was reaching puberty and used her for sexual experimentation. Those years are clouded in her memory, but she does remember that it was a confusing time for her and that she blamed herself for the abuse. She repressed the memories until, as a college student, she entered a physical relationship with a young man. Then the abuse memories came rushing back, and she went into a period of deep depression and sorrow. She spent her own days in bed, as her mother had done, and began failing classes and resorting to drugs and alcohol to numb her pain. She was lost and broken.

During this time, she met a young woman in one of her classes who invited her to her home. Abigail accepted the invitation, and immediately could see that this family was quite different from hers. They ate dinner together, spent time together, talked nightly, and went to Mass together. Every evening, the mother excused herself from the others and retreated to a corner of their living room. Using Bible prayer cards and rosaries, she'd spend thirty to sixty minutes in prayer. Abigail had never seen anybody with such faith! One day, she got up the courage to ask the woman to teach her how to pray. She gave Abigail a pamphlet on the Rosary—the first time Abigail understood the real meaning and method of this prayer. She also gave her a prayer card to St. Thérèse (The Little Flower), which she still has.

Her friend's mother also insisted that, if Abigail slept over on a Saturday night, she'd be required to attend Mass with them on Sunday mornings. "That was probably the greatest gift she ever gave me," Abigail wrote. "Though it still would be a while before Jesus was able to turn all that pain and sorrow into joy. My friend's mother was only planting a seed."

Abigail continued to be plagued by anxiety attacks and bouts of depression. She spent many years in therapy but still was very broken. Her self-esteem hadn't recovered from her childhood abuse, and she was constantly overcome with fear. She was petrified that she would die and be condemned to hell. She never achieved her career dreams. In time, she married and had children, but her brokenness put her marriage on shaky ground. She loved her children and loved being a mother but struggled to be motherly. She didn't want to regenerate the cycles of her parents, but she hadn't the skills or tools to do otherwise.

Twenty years after her friend's mother had reintroduced Abigail to the Catholic faith, she was invited to a Bible study. She went, albeit reluctantly. In the Bible study, she learned that God loved her and that fathers aren't always scary. She learned that her heavenly Father wanted what was best for her and had promised never to fail or abandon her. She grew in understanding God's word and returned to regular reception of the sacraments. Her knowledge of God's love transformed her; what she once had done out of obligation she now did out of ardent desire.

Within the sacrament of reconciliation, she was able to shift the blame to where it really belonged and see herself as a worthy, lovable person.

"In the sacrament of reconciliation, I felt that Jesus sat with me, held my hand, and listened to me," she wrote. "My tears brought healing. I was forgiven for those things that I was indeed guilty of and was shown where the guilt truthfully was mine. The Lord forgave me and had made me free!"

Abigail sought spiritual direction. That along with the graces of a sacramental life changed her heart completely. Revisiting the horrible memories is indeed difficult, but she's different now and she realizes that. Her abusers also were somehow changed. They now go to her for counsel, guidance, and love. Because of her transformation, Abigail is able to embrace them all, see each of them as a child of God, and recognize that their past—and present—behavior stemmed from their own brokenness.

One day as she was walking, Abigail conversed with God, asking him why he had given her the family that he did. She didn't understand why God allowed the abuse, especially since she hadn't deserved it. A still small voice in her heart said, "I did not give them to you for you, I gave them to you for them." This moment was an epiphany for Abigail, and she realized that she'd be made stronger and wiser through her sufferings.

"[God] would use the joy I discovered in the sacraments to not only heal me, but to heal each of them in some way," she wrote. "Furthermore, God knew I would then go forth and be used through my work to heal other people in the same situations. As St. Paul tells us, whatever you have been comforted in, God will then use to comfort others in. My sorrow has truly been turned to joy."

Abigail's story is a remarkable example of finding healing in the sacraments. It's also remarkable in that she saw her friend's mother as the instrument who led her to the sacraments and that she realizes she has now become an instrument for others to find the sacraments.

My personal conviction is that people turn to addictions—drugs, alcohol, sexual behavior, pornography—and thrill-seeking behavior because what they really hunger for is God. The "high" of the drugs, alcohol, sex, and thrills supplants the real high of God's grace and abundant love. Because of our brokenness, we often forget or don't realize that we already *have* God's love. All we need to do is open our hearts and accept it! But we don't, because we don't believe in the power of his love, and all too often we don't believe that we're worthy of it either.

That's why the sacrament of reconciliation is so vital to our growing in the love of God. It's in the confessional that we can let go of our own sins and our resentment of the sins of others so that we'll be free to love God with all our heart.

This is how Abigail moved from sorrow to joy. Plainly, it was not easy, nor did it happen quickly. It won't be that way for you (or me) either. But it will *be* at some point, because Jesus promised that he is the Bread from heaven that gives life to the world. In our sorrow, we must cling to the sacraments for our own healing and for the healing of others. Sometimes, that's all we have—the next confession, the next Eucharist—to look forward to. And that's okay, as long as we do keep looking forward to them. Beyond doubt, our Lord is present in all the sacraments. He's there in the confessional listening to you, hurting with you, and ready to forgive your sins and open your heart to forgive others' sins. He's there in Eucharistic Adoration, waiting for you to pour your heart out to him. He's present in the Eucharist, eager to unite his Presence with yours. Abigail's example demonstrates the reality of the sacraments and their power to transform.

Ask *and* YOU SHALL RECEIVE

"And I tell you, ask and you will receive; seek and you will find; knock and the door will be opened to you. For everyone who asks, receives; and the one who seeks, finds; and to the one who knocks, the door will be opened. What father among you would hand his son a snake when he asks for a fish? Or hand him a scorpion when he asks for an egg? If you then, who are wicked, know how to give good gifts to your children, how much more will the Father in heaven give the holy Spirit to those who ask him?"

LUKE 11:9–13

I remember wanting a bicycle when I was a child. I didn't know how to ride yet, but that didn't matter to me. I'd figure it out somehow. Learning to ride a bike was far less intimidating to me than asking my parents to give me one, however. I was afraid they'd say "no." I knew I'd have to ask in just the right way so that they'd be convinced I really *needed* a bike. I spent a lot of time fretting, procrastinating, and figuring out how to ask. Finally, I got up the nerve to launch the question to my folks. It worked, sort of. They didn't say no, but they didn't say yes, either. They said they'd think about it. Well, after a time, I got a bike, but not the brand-new, colorful banana seat, high handlebar one I saw in the store. One day my dad presented me with a sturdy, used bike with regular handlebars and seat. It was grass green. Ugh.

My initial reaction to that bike was shameful. Not only was I ungrateful, but I even became angry at my parents for getting that one instead of the one I really wanted (and pompously felt I deserved). I'm embarrassed to admit that I wasn't very nice to them that day, and for many days after I refused to so much as look at it. But my yearning to ride overran my displeasure with the bike. Since I had no choice—I certainly didn't have the means to get my dream bike on my own—I decided to make the best of what I considered was a crummy situation.

It didn't take long for me to discover that the bike I'd been given was in truth perfect for me. Not the most agile kid, I struggled with learning how to ride it. I tried and tried, both with help and on my own, but just couldn't get the knack. There were plenty of scrapes and dings (on both the bike and me) to drive home the point that giving a flashy new bike to someone who hadn't yet acquired the skills would have been imprudent. There was another advantage too. The older bike had wider tires and was easier to balance than a new one. The ugly, old, green one was easier to learn to ride. Eventually, I got the hang of it. I started thinking that it wasn't such a bad bike after all, even though it wasn't as fancy as the bikes some of my neighborhood friends were riding. I stopped being mad at my folks for getting me the "wrong" bike and better appreciated the "right" bike for me.

I got a bike, albeit not the bike I originally wanted, but the bike that was good for me to have. Why? Because I had the courage to ask. This is a very human example of the way we approach—or fail to approach—the heavenly Father for the desires of our hearts. We're afraid to ask for what we want or need because we fear the answer will be "no." Or, we worry that we'll receive something we didn't want or hadn't bargained for. Sometimes, we halfheartedly ask because we doubt God's goodness or capability to grant our request. What's the use of asking when he's not going to give us what we want, anyway? Too often, we give up on asking because the answer is too long in coming.

It's especially hard when we're steeped in sorrow. Whether we sorrow over our own situation or the situation of someone we care for, we can become discouraged and reticent to ask—or keep asking—for the sorrow to be turned to joy. To ask in the first place, to believe in God's power to provide for us, to continue asking even when all seems lost—all this requires courage.

Deb Hadley had the courage to ask and to keep asking. She trusted in God's providence and in the power of the Holy Spirit to guide her. That might not seem like such a big deal until you learn that Deb lost two young adult children within a single year. She twice endured the horror that no mother wants to face and yet discovered within herself a stronger faith that led her to help strengthen the faith of others.

DEB HADLEY: PRAY CONTINUALLY

The death of Deb's daughter, Kaylie, devastated her. In her own words, "It almost killed me." Kaylie died on June 5, 2013, just before her twenty-fifth birthday. Kaylie resigned from her position teaching high school English, Speech, and Theater and was in the process of moving back home to teach summer school and plan her January 25, 2014 wedding. She never arrived home.

Diagnosed in 2010 with epilepsy, Kaylie had experienced a number of grand mal seizures. They usually occurred as she was waking up from sleep, and she was taking medication to control them. On the day of her death, Kaylie must have laid down to take a nap before her long drive home and had a seizure upon waking. The seizure claimed her life, and she died of cardiac arrest. (This is known as SUDEP—Sudden Unexpected Death from Epilepsy, a condition when a person's epilepsy is well controlled and yet he or she dies for no apparent reason.)

"I was in complete shock," Deb wrote. "I didn't know what to do with my emotions. I couldn't wrap my mind around what was happening. How can you speak with someone every single day of your life and then they are gone? Where are they? At that moment, I didn't know who God was, where Kaylie was, or how I would live."

Grief-stricken, Deb couldn't eat, drink, or sleep and became so paranoid that she was unable to leave the house. She was emotionally and physically sick and experienced indescribable physical pain. She lost her desire to live, even to the point of considering various methods of suicide. The only thing that stopped her was the fear of ending up being disabled rather than dead and the pain and trauma it would inflict on her family. She prayed ardently that the Second Coming would happen soon so that she wouldn't have to live anymore. She planned her funeral, bought additional life insurance, and told all her friends that when she died, it would be a celebration.

Despite having been quite active in her parish, Deb didn't really understand who God was. She describes herself at that time in her life as a "Surface Catholic." She knew that she needed to cling to God if she was going to get through this. She began attending Mass daily, studying Scripture, surrounding herself with people who could help her grow in her faith, and going to women's faith conferences. Her faith deepened and her relationship with God changed from a superficial one to one of profound love and trust.

She was away from home at a women's faith conference on March 7, 2014, when she heard there was a bad car accident in a nearby town. She called her twenty-year-old son, Tyler, to assure herself that he hadn't been involved. He didn't answer his phone. Panicked, Deb called the town's police station to inquire and was told by the dispatcher that four boys had passed away in the accident and that Tyler had been one of them. She forced the dispatcher to reveal the names of the other three boys so that she could pray for them. Then she hung up the phone.

"I woke up the entire hotel," she wrote. "I kept yelling, 'Oh, my God. Oh, my God.' I could not wrap my head around what was happening. I couldn't comprehend it. I knew I couldn't live. I knew that I could not go through this again."

Deb's sister-in-law drove her home from the conference, and as Deb rode, she prayed for God's help. Then she thanked him for his infinite love. Deep inside, she trusted him and knew that he would indeed help her. Somehow, she understood that her experience with Kaylie had prepared her for this moment.

"[With Kaylie's death] I was the grieving mother. For Tyler, I had to be the rock that everyone needed, as four boys were gone, four families were devastated, and their friends were beside themselves. I prayed with everyone. I gave hope to everyone," she explained.

By grace alone, Deb was able to speak at Tyler's funeral, assuring those present that God would get them through the ordeal and that good would come from it. She describes this as "a total Holy Spirit moment." She believes the Holy Spirit also was the reason she was able to speak to a group of Tyler's classmates and friends the day after his funeral.

For more than a decade, Deb had a strange sense that God had an important task in mind for her. It came to her during a Bible study, but she never acted on it. After Kaylie's death, she started a Facebook page called RIP Angel Kaylie as an outlet for her emotions. After Tyler's death, she changed the name to RIP Angel Tyler Kaylie. The page showed her how badly people were hungering for God's word and something to fill their emptiness. RIP Angel Tyler Kaylie gained nearly four thousand followers in a very short time.

Finally, the task God had for her became evident. She understood now that she was called to share her story publicly and through it lead others to Christ. She took a professional speaking class and began marketing herself as a presenter. Parallel to the public speaking, Deb was urged to start the KT Humble Hearts Foundation, an organization dedicated to raising funds for school scholarships, for epilepsy research, and for families in grief or hardship.

Deb's sorrow had turned to joy.

"I knew the love that the Lord has for me," she said. "My joy came through the incredible people God has brought into my life, the doors that have opened, the healing that has happened in me, and the healing I see in others. I know that I am to shine God's love on all I meet and that one day God will bring me home! Until then, I'll embrace each day the Lord has given me."

Ask and you will receive; seek and you will find; knock, and the door will be opened to you. That's what Jesus told his disciples, and that's exactly what Deb Hadley did. No doubt she would rather have had Tyler and Kaylie alive again, but that simply was not possible. Instead, she asked for God's guidance and help to overcome her grief and to heal from the trauma. Her life is still hard without her two beloved children, and she's easily moved to tears when remembering them. Nothing will replace their loss. But God showed Deb a way to use her pain to ease the pain of others.

It's not easy to heal from a devastating loss. At such a time, you can feel as though God has abandoned you. Maybe you, like Deb, have wished to die. Hurt, anger, fear, and confusion can overwhelm you and lead you to distance yourself from God. This is exactly the point at which you need to turn *toward* God and ask him—perhaps many times over—to help you to trust in him.

Nothing is concealed *that* will not be revealed

"Therefore do not be afraid of them. Nothing is concealed that will not be revealed, nor secret that will not be known. What I say to you in the darkness, speak in the light; what you hear whispered, proclaim on the housetops. And do not be afraid of those who kill the body but cannot kill the soul; rather, be afraid of the one who can destroy both soul and body in Gehenna. Are not two sparrows sold for a small coin? Yet not one of them falls to the ground without your Father's knowledge. Even all the hairs of your head are counted. So do not be afraid; you are worth more than many sparrows." MATTHEW 10:26–31

When someone tells you a secret, they expect you not to share it with others. In this Scripture passage, our Lord expects just the opposite.

"What I say to you in the darkness, speak in the light; what you hear whispered, proclaim on the housetops."

That seems counterintuitive to our experience of things being said in the dark. Generally, things spoken in darkness are best kept in darkness. Jesus, however, tells us the opposite. This line of Scripture kept me puzzled for years and years. Then one day it occurred to me: Jesus says to utter in the light that which *he* tells us in the dark. He doesn't say to utter in the light what anyone *else* tells us in the dark. There's a huge difference!

There was a time when I was in a situation with no apparent way out. I was the subject of gossip, prying into my private affairs, and false judgments, and there was no effective way to defend myself. Unless I abandoned my entire life as it was— which was not a feasible option—there was no escape. I was close to despair. Stuck in this darkness, I couldn't see my way out. I didn't even know how to pray about it.

One day, I sat tearfully before our Lord in Eucharistic Adoration. My heart was empty, my mind was frazzled, and I was physically exhausted. Still, I wanted to "be" before Jesus, darkness and all. I tried to pray, but it was useless. So, I just sat there. Finally, the only thing I could bring myself to say was, "Lord, I have no idea what to do with this. I want to just quit." I sat there some more, looking at the monstrance and waiting. Suddenly, the words came to me, *And do not fear those who kill the body but cannot kill the soul; rather fear him who can destroy both soul and body in hell.* Then, I understood. Perhaps my adversaries could cause harm to my reputation or circumstances, but they could not harm my soul. As God's precious child, I had nothing truly to fear from them. I only had to fear what the evil one could do to me if I succumbed to sinfulness. All I had to do was be sure I was right with God and follow his will for me. What I heard Jesus say to me in my darkness, I knew I had to utter in the light and proclaim from the housetops.

That experience during Adoration has completely changed me. Sure, I feel the darkness creep back from time to time. But, when it does, I go back to Jesus's promise: *So have no fear of them; for nothing is concealed that will not be revealed, or hidden that will not be known.* What Jesus whispers to us in our darkness, we share in the light so that we can witness to his goodness and be a source of encouragement for others.

Darlene[11] knows what it's like to be whispered to in the darkness. And she knows what it's like to proclaim it from the housetops. Losing both of her legs from mid-calf down, she never wavered in her faith and never questioned God's goodness. She knew that she need not fear those who can kill the body, for her soul will rise with Jesus.

---

11 Not her real name.

DARLENE: THE LIGHT AT THE END

One night, Darlene became very ill for no apparent reason. She was so ill, in fact, that her husband, Randy,[12] took her to the hospital. At the hospital, she was told she had kidney stones, was given pain medication, and released. The medication, the doctor said, would help her endure the pain until the stones had passed.

Two days later, Randy returned Darlene to the hospital deathly ill. The staff ran blood tests but noticed nothing in the results and sent her back home. At home, she became increasingly ill, required re-hospitalization, and slipped into a coma that lasted fourteen days. During that time, her father anointed her with oil and prayed, "Dear God, please do not let my daughter die." Gangrene set into her lower legs, and while she was yet comatose, the doctors amputated both legs at mid-calf. Eventually, she managed to come out of the coma and recover from her mysterious illness. With the help of prostheses, she was able to learn to walk again. But her life would never be the same.

Friends encouraged Darlene to sue for malpractice, but she didn't believe in it. She felt that everyone makes mistakes, and she wanted to forgive the hospital's oversights and move on. However, prostheses are costly—upwards of $30,000 per set—and she and Randy didn't have the means for her medical costs. Then some facts came to light. Randy, an FBI agent, thought to take copies of the hospital records with him when Darlene was released. Additionally, one of the nurses later confided to Darlene and Randy that, an hour after Darlene

---

12 Not his real name.

left the hospital the first time, the staff reviewed her blood tests and discovered that she had had bile in her bloodstream. She should have been called and told to return immediately to the hospital, but that call was never made. No one knows who made the decision to lay aside those critical blood test results.

The malpractice mediation took place in the state capital, a plane ride away from Darlene's home. Also on the plane were ten doctors named in the lawsuit. While on the plane, all ten wore sports jackets or suits, dress shirts, and ties. When they walked into the mediation room, however, they wore hospital smocks in protest of Darlene having worn a skirt that showed her prostheses, when she normally wore long, billowing slacks. The emergency room doctor who was on duty the night of Darlene's first crisis was seated across the table from her. His head hung down, and it was obvious to Darlene that the hospital intended for him to take all of the blame for the malpractice. Her heart broke for him, and so when it was her turn to testify, she refused to allow the line of questioning to point the blame entirely on the emergency room doctor. In the end, Darlene won the case and was given a settlement. Since winning the malpractice suit, Darlene has testified before Congress and her state legislature about malpractice caps.

She's gone on to live a full life, ministering to others in similar difficulties. "You are terribly alone if you do not find others who have experienced what you are experiencing," she wrote. She remembers leaving the hospital in a wheelchair being pushed by her husband. "My eyes searched everywhere, back and forth, looking for someone who might have a prosthetic leg so I could talk to them." She's learned to draw strength from those who have preceded her in having legs amputated. She especially remembers the therapist who worked with her when she was being fitted for her prostheses. The man kept encouraging her that she "could do this." When she wondered why he was so positive, he pulled up his pants leg to show her his own prosthetic leg.

Of course, she has her sad moments, but overall Darlene has maintained a positive attitude that she credits to her faith. She wrote, "Every day when I wake up it is my choice: 'Am I going to put on my grumpy face or ask God how he wants to use me today?' The choice is mine." She went on to say, "I do not believe God planned this for me, but I do believe he can use it in my life and in the lives of others. Faith is the light at the end of the tunnel for me."

Darlene has allowed the loss of her legs to become a blessing and not a curse—for herself and others. She is here in order to serve God in whatever capacity she is able. "I would not have chosen to lose my legs, but I cannot deny that God has done some special things in my life because of losing my legs," she wrote.

So have no fear of them; for nothing is concealed that will not be revealed, or hidden that will not be known. Our Lord said this to his disciples, he said it to Darlene, he said it to me, and he's saying it to you right now. Who is the "them" you are not to fear? Certainly, it's evil people and situations. But also, you are not to fear tragedies, traumas, betrayals, confusion, accidents, abuses, addictions, illnesses, hardships, or even the day-to-day difficulties that can weigh you down and make you worry. "Them" is anything that shakes your confidence in God or makes you question his wisdom. "Them" is whatever can kill the body and soul in hell. Fear not, for even the hairs on your head are numbered. What he has whispered to you in the darkness will be proclaimed in the light.

Whatever you ask *in* my name, I will do it

"Amen, amen, I say to you, whoever believes in me will do the works that I do, and will do greater ones than these, because I am going to the Father. And whatever you ask in my name, I will do, so that the Father may be glorified in the Son. If you ask anything of me in my name, I will do it."

JOHN 14:12–14

F or decades, I prayed the same prayer without receiving an answer—or at least not the answer I wanted. My prayer was for my mother's healing from mental illness and her return to the Church. Her illness caused her to be abusive, and my siblings and I still bear scars from our experiences with her. I began my prayer on the day my father died, when I was just fifteen years old. The only one of us four children who still lived at home, I expected that living alone with my mother would mean I'd bear the brunt of her abusiveness. I was quite right. I've written about this more fully in my book *Forgiving Mother: A Marian Novena of Healing and Peace*,[13] but for now it's enough to say that my only recourse in that dire situation was to pray. Never knowing what would come at me when or from where in terms of my mother's behavior, I could only ask our Lord for his protection for me and the grace of healing and conversion for my mother.

I moved out as soon as I could, attending college in another city. Soon, I met a wonderful young man, married him, and together we had four children of our own. During all this time, I tried to be a charitable daughter by keeping contact with and occasionally visiting my mother. But, through phone calls and vicious letters, the long arm of her abusiveness kept reaching further. When the calls and letters reached toward my children, I had to completely cut off contact with my mother. Yet, I never gave up praying, asking in Jesus' name, for my mother's healing and conversion. I begged the Blessed Virgin Mary for her intercession for my mother's healing, and protection

---

13 *Forgiving Mother: A Marian Novena of Healing and Peace*, by Marge Steinhage Fenelon, ©2017, Servant Books.

and healing for myself. I can honestly say that Mary has been the only real mother I have ever known.

More than ten years after I distanced myself from my mother, my brother discovered that some kind people had moved her into an assisted living facility and that she'd definitely aged, but her health was stable. Our initial efforts to reconnect were met with hostility and so we backed off. A few years later, we found out that my mother's health had begun to decline and that she'd been moved to the facility's medical unit. This time, reconnecting went better. My mother had entered the beginning stages of dementia and her abusiveness abated. It was possible to have pleasant visits with my mother, and so my husband and I made the drive to see her a few times a year. As the dementia progressed, we visited more often. Before long, my mother had stopped eating, and the facility staff knew that the end would come soon. At every visit, I asked my mother to pray with me, or at least listen as I prayed the Rosary beside her bed. She would have none of it. I asked her to please accept a visit from the local parish priest, and she adamantly refused. My prayers became desperate. What would happen if she died without turning back to God? Without receiving the last rites?[14]

---

14 In the Catholic Church, the "last rites" consist of the sacrament of the anointing of the sick and viaticum. In anointing of the sick, the person who is ill receives the special grace of the uniting of the sick person to the passion of Christ, for his own good and that of the whole Church; the strengthening, peace, and courage to endure in a Christian manner the sufferings of illness or old age; the forgiveness of sins, if the sick person was not able to obtain it through the sacrament of penance; the restoration

The call came one morning as I worked in my home office. It was the facility's social worker, telling me that my mother had passed away peacefully in her sleep sometime between midnight and 1AM. As far as she knew, no priest had visited my mother and she had not received last rites. I was completely crushed. I knew that the grave sinfulness my mother had lived in for much of her life and her turning from the Church put her in danger of losing eternity unless she had converted on her deathbed. Sadly, that didn't seem to have happened. Despite the things my mother had done, I still wanted her to be happy with Jesus in heaven. She had donated her body to science, so there wouldn't even be a funeral.

Two days later, another call came from the social worker. "I knew you'd want to know this," she said. "I just found out that your mother *did* receive last rites. A priest came to visit her on Memorial Day and administered the sacraments to her. She received Communion before she died."

I was ecstatic beyond words, and I sat dumbfounded for a spell. I asked the social worker to repeat her message so that I could be sure I had heard correctly. Yes, I had heard right. My mother had turned back to God before she died. I had asked, in Jesus' name, and he did what I asked. My decades of deep sorrow had turned to a fountain of joy.

---

of health, if it is conducive to the salvation of his soul and the preparation for passing over to eternal life. Viaticum is the Eucharist given to the dying person at the moment of his "passing over" to the Father. (See *Catechism of the Catholic Church*, 1524 and 1532.)

If you ask anything in Jesus' name, he will do it. That is his promise to you, to all of us. He doesn't always act exactly in the way that you would want or expect, but he *does* act.

Author and speaker Maureen Pratt has suffered with chronic illness for nearly her entire life. Would she prefer not to have these painful and sometimes debilitating conditions? Of course. Yet she accepts them and bears them gratefully as both a gift and mission from God. She prays in Jesus' name, asking for the strength and courage to move forward, serving God the best she can one day at a time. And in return, Jesus gives her the grace to carry on with her mission of serving and inspiring others. I must say, she does an exceptional job of it! In her years of writing, teaching, and giving presentations, she has led countless people closer to our Lord and to a greater appreciation of the challenges they have been given.

I had the privilege of interviewing her for this book. Her answers to my questions were a reflection of the grace and wisdom our Lord has bestowed on her in her own suffering and in her ministry to ease the suffering of others.

MAUREEN PRATT: GIVE JESUS A CHANCE

Maureen has been catastrophically ill her whole life. She nearly had to repeat first grade because she'd missed too many days of school. She had pneumonia thirteen times before she was eighteen years old and was given last rites in the hospital because she was allergic to penicillin and sulfa drugs. She says that, humanly speaking, she should be dead right now. There were times when she was confined to bed for weeks at a time with pneumonia, isolated from friends, and unable to attend school. For as long as she can remember, she's lived in chronic pain. Finally, eighteen years ago, she was diagnosed with lupus. Her physical appearance changed, her body changed, and her life stopped being as she had known it. Looking back, she believes that she probably has had lupus all her life. However, when she was a child, pediatric lupus was little understood and difficult to diagnose. It's a disease that still is not well understood.

Maureen's life indeed has been a struggle, yet she's never become angry or resentful about it. "I hear many Christians say that God doesn't want me to be sick. He only wants the best for me and the best for me is to not be sick," she said. "Well, Jesus died on a cross, and to say that we with chronic pain and illness are not supposed to be sick is to completely denigrate what Christ did on the cross, which was to suffer and die. In the Garden, he prayed to his Father, 'please take this cup from me.' It's a very human gesture. But then he said, 'not my will but your will be done.' I believe that God can cure us at any moment, and miraculous cures do happen. But how realistic is it for us to never have problems in our lives?"

This realization led Maureen to accept her pain and illness as a way to draw closer to Jesus. She refrained from wondering *why me?* and instead told herself, *why not me?* Once she had made that conscious decision, she was able to move forward in her life.

"A lot of people with chronic pain and illness are stuck," she said. "They repeatedly circle back to the same problem—my family doesn't understand, my doctor doesn't understand me, I feel so alone, and so on. You've seen how a dog will circle and circle and circle until there is nothing left of their bed but the bottom of the floor. We do that when we have chronic pain and illness sometimes, too. We circle and circle and circle, we can't just plop ourselves down and come to God in prayer or lift ourselves up to God. So, to me, living with chronic pain and illness—and I have many disabilities—is hard, but it is a call to be active. That can take many forms, but it's the first step toward feeling Jesus' comfort."

Maureen took solace in daily Scripture reading, especially the New Testament. It allowed her to consider what Jesus did and said and to see how humanly Jesus had lived. She took great comfort in his story of teaching, suffering, death and resurrection. The more she got to know Jesus, the better she felt. It led her to wholeheartedly say, "Not my will, but thy will be done." She also advocates spontaneous prayer, which she uses often to express her helplessness and sorrow to God.

Maureen doesn't see joy and sorrow as mutually exclusive. There wasn't a particular moment when her sorrow turned to joy, but rather it's been a process through which there was joy amid the sorrow. She's found her joy in calling upon God in her suffering and receiving his gifts and consolations in return.

"We have a loving Father," she said. "God loves us, and he wants us to be closer to him. He wants us to feel his support and encouragement in our discomfort. The only thing preventing us from feeling that is ourselves. There is no need to think that you can't feel closer to God because he wants you to be closer to him. He's waiting there and he's never absent. We call on him and he opens his arms."

Maureen is right. Joy and sorrow aren't mutually exclusive. Joy isn't a happy-go-lucky feeling, as though you haven't a care in the world. Joy is deeper, more profound, and long-term. Joy, when seen in the context of the Eternal, is everlasting! You can be struck by a terrible tragedy and still be joyful, knowing that, no matter how bad things may be, God is in control and Jesus will never abandon you. Joy is what lifts you up, tucks you into the heavenly Father's arms, and carries you through the most difficult of times.

There is a paragraph from Maureen's book *Peace in the Storm* that is so powerful that I want to share it with you:

> You need to call upon the Lord.
>
> Look inward and breathe deeply. Ask for strength.
>
> *Do not be afraid or discouraged, for the Lord is the one who goes before you. He will be with you; he will neither fail nor forsake you.*
>
> The Lord is more powerful than all our fears combined. He created you and me. He is with us through everything, through every step on our journey to the summit of the mountain.[15]

That is true joy!

---

15 *Peace in the Storm: Meditations on Chronic Pain and Illness,* Image Books, 2005, p. 9.

There is another passage—this one from her book *Beyond Pain: Job, Jesus, and Joy*, that I'd like to share with you as well.

> The joy that Jesus brings is far beyond any that we experience on earth. It is a divine joy that culminates in the reality of the Resurrection, the Lord's promise fulfilled. We still need strength, courage, and self-awareness to build our faith and ministry. But we have Jesus' light to guide us and his example to follow. This is a tall order, especially if we are physically and emotionally frail. But, as we know, nothing is impossible with God...[16]

Whether your sorrow is caused by physical, mental, emotional, situational, or financial hardships, God is more powerful than any trouble you may face, any obstacle you meet with, any woe that weighs you down. He knows your suffering and wants to help you, but he will not force his way into your heart. He awaits your invitation. Invite him! Our Lord knows what is best for you—even when the best is something very, very hard for you—and he will see to it that you have the guidance and grace that you need to fulfill God's will for you.

Recall what Jesus said in the Scripture passage at the beginning of this chapter. He said, "*he who believes in me will also do the works that I do; and greater works than these will he do...*" Jesus doesn't specify *how* you will do those works, or *what* works they will be. But, he does guarantee that, if you have faith in him, whatever works you do will be great.

------

16 *Beyond Pain: Job, Jesus, and Joy*, Twenty-Third Publications, 2010, p. 62.

COME *to* ME...
and I WILL GIVE
YOU REST

"Come to me, all you who labor and are burdened, and I will give you rest. Take my yoke upon you and learn from me, for I am meek and humble of heart; and you will find rest for yourselves. For my yoke is easy, and my burden light." MATTHEW 11:28-30

There is an interesting aspect of this Scripture passage that I think is often overlooked. In it, our Lord offers rest to those who carry heavy burdens, but in no way does he say that he will take those burdens away. Instead, he asks us to take his yoke upon ourselves and learn from him. The kind of yoke Jesus is referring to is the kind that is used for oxen when they are working in the fields, threshing grain, or pulling weighty carts. The yoke is laid on the shoulders of two oxen at once in an arrangement that requires them to work together to complete the work. Either they work together, or the whole thing turns into chaos. Jesus' invitation to us is to take our place in his yoke— we on the one side and he on the other. Thus, we're required to work together with him or everything will fall into chaos. If we try to wear the yoke alone, nothing will get done. If we pull the yoke along with our Lord, things really start moving. This is what Jesus is explaining to us in the Scripture passage.

But there's more. Jesus isn't only asking us to take our place beside him; he also is assuring us that his yoke is easy and his burden is light. Does that mean that our Lord doesn't carry much of a burden? Not at all. We know from the New Testament passages about his work and ministry that Jesus certainly did not have an easy go of it. Once he left Joseph and Mary's home, he traversed the hot, dry countryside of Israel and Palestine, teaching, preaching, and healing. I've been there and know firsthand that it was some pretty rugged territory to travel on foot! Additionally, Jesus did not have a home of his own during those years—not even a place to lay his head, as he told the scribe who pledged to follow him wherever he went (Mt 8:20). Clearly, our Lord did not live a life of leisure. Throughout his ministry, Jesus was harassed by hecklers, skeptics, and accusers who wanted nothing more than to see him dead. Before long, that wish became reality when Jesus was arrested, imprisoned, scourged, taunted, crowned with thorns, and forced to carry an unmanageable cross through the streets of Jerusalem and up the hill of Calvary. Finally, he was nailed to that cross and died an excruciating, prolonged, and gruesome death. That, indeed, was an extremely heavy burden!

Is our Lord asking us to carry that same heavy burden? Yes. And no. For sure we will have burdens to carry, and those burdens will become cumbersome at times. But, because we have taken our place on the other side of Jesus' yoke, even the most unwieldy of burdens will seem light because we carry it beside our Lord and Savior. That is Jesus' promise to us. We never, ever, will carry any burden alone if we allow ourselves to be yoked beside Jesus.

This is exactly what happened to Bethany[17]. She was given an unimaginably heavy burden when her teenage son tried to commit suicide. In the beginning, it seemed as though the burden's weight was simply too much for her. Then, one day, the yoke unexpectedly became lighter. She had stopped trying

---

17 Not her real name.

to carry it on her own and began allowing Jesus to take up his place beside her.

BETHANY: A SWORD PIERCED MY HEART

It was a beautiful, sunny fall day in September 2009. Bethany was in the kitchen, getting the family's day started and seeing them off to work and school. She said goodbye to her seventeen-year-old son, Jay,[18] and asked if he'd be home for supper. Holding his cell phone in his hand and with a look of determination on his face, he assured her that he would be.

A few minutes later, Bethany got a call from Jay's girlfriend. "Jay is going to the fertilizer plant building; he says he's going to jump off!"

Bethany was struck with a fear that gripped her heart and tore at its very fibers. Feigning calmness, she arranged for the neighbor to stay with her two younger sons so she could drive to the scene where Jay was attempting suicide. She called 911, reporting what she knew and requesting police to be dispatched to the area. She prayed fervently to anybody in heaven whom she thought might care enough to stop him.

As she got closer to the fertilizer plant, she saw Jay's tall, thin silhouette eight stories high, on top of the abandoned building. He had threatened suicide eight months earlier but hadn't gone through with it. Bethany expected that this time would be the same. This time, though, she vowed to herself that she would have him admitted as an inpatient at the psychiatric hospital.

---

18 Not his real name.

As she drew nearer, she saw a multitude of police cars, fire trucks, and an ambulance. *Why so many?* she thought to herself as she pulled up to the gate.

She pleaded with the police officers blocking the gate to let her in. They seemed unmoved.

"I'm his mother! Where is he? Let me in!" she begged.

Then she heard the words that no mother wants to hear. "He jumped off. He's in the ambulance."

Bethany fell to the ground, unable to comprehend and unwilling to believe the words she'd just heard. She was sure Jay was dead.

"Your son is alive and is being taken to the children's hospital," one officer said. "He called 911 and said that his jaw hurt."

She couldn't imagine that there was any way that Jay had survived the jump.

Bethany wanted to follow the ambulance in her car, but the police wouldn't allow her to drive. As she rode, she thought of the calls she'd have to make—her husband, Jay's older sister and brother, Jay's grandparents. She'd have to listen to their gasps and shocked silence. She had decisions to make and care to arrange for her younger sons. She couldn't make her phone work and had to call numbers several times as her fingers fumbled.

Once all the family members had arrived at the hospital, they were hurried off to a private waiting room. They huddled together and braced themselves for the tragic words that Jay had died. But that's not what they heard. The staff told them that Jay was alive and didn't have any life-threatening injuries that could be detected. There was no internal bleeding, but there were multiple skull fractures, yet no brain damage. He had a broken clavicle and one broken vertebra, but still had feeling in his legs. Jay's family knew that they had been given both a miracle and a heavy cross.

A nurse invited Bethany to go to Jay's room to see him. As she entered, he commanded her to leave in an angry, threatening tone. He didn't want his mother; he didn't want to be alive. It was as if a solid door had bolted shut in Bethany's face. It would be years before Jay would finally let his mother in.

In one tragic moment, the family's lives had been changed forever. Bethany describes their new life as akin to riding a raft down a foaming, raging, deep canyon river.

Jay was in the children's hospital for four weeks and had three surgeries. Two repaired the extensive skull fractures, and a tracheotomy allowed him to breathe, as the swelling in his head could block his windpipe. Fortunately, his nose, teeth, eyes, and brain were not damaged at all. Bethany remembers staring in disbelief at Jay's swollen head, looking at his knees and other exposed skin, and wondering why there weren't any cuts or bruises. Her husband had gotten more scrapes and bruises from a fall off his bike than Jay had gotten from his jump off an 80-foot high building.

During Jay's hospital stay, Bethany felt the presence of God, and she sensed that her suffering Savior was accompanying her in her own suffering. Even though she felt as though she was falling apart inside, she could bring herself to pray, and in that she was sustained. Countless people prayed for the family, and there was a steady stream of visitors. She especially found comfort and strength in our Lord's Mother, Mary, because she understood what it was like to watch a son suffer pain. Like Mary, a sword had pierced Bethany's heart. Her heart literally ached for Jay, for his incomprehensible pain—both physical and emotional. There were many signs of comfort, guidance, and love, and from these signs she received a quiet, patient strength that was not of herself. The family received overwhelming support from extended family, friends, hospital staff, doctors, coworkers, Jay's friends, and their priest. They were a tangible sign of an intangible God. They were his hands, his voice, his eyes, his love made manifest, and Bethany was incredibly grateful for them all.

Though she rejoiced at every small victory in Jay's healing process, Bethany also feared it. While he was bound to his bed by medical equipment and had a nursing assistant assigned to monitor him around the clock, she knew Jay was safe. Each step toward less care meant that they were one day closer to his admittance to an adolescent psychiatric hospital and subsequent release to home. Then Bethany would be responsible for keeping him alive. Clearly, Jay was upset that he had survived, and this was made worse because of the deep remorse he felt for the pain he caused his family and friends. On top of that, Jay lacked self-confidence, avoided conflict, and buried his negative feelings. All of this made recovering from a suicide attempt more challenging.

The adolescent psychiatric hospital to which Jay was moved was more than an hour away from the family home. He hated being there and pleaded with Bethany to get him out as soon as possible. His stay lasted two weeks and included a series of individual and family counseling sessions through which a safety plan was devised for when Jay would be released. Trust had to be reestablished and that was hard on everyone. Sadly, there were no support groups for parents of children who had survived suicide—only for those who had not. At the time Jay had attempted suicide, Bethany had thought he was doing well, but she was mistaken. She couldn't afford to make the same mistake twice.

In the year following, Bethany lived in a constant state of fright. She was never certain that Jay was all right, and she was prone to sudden bouts of terror. Panic gripped her stomach every time the phone rang. The sound of sirens would make her frantic and she'd weep uncontrollably. Whenever she approached Jay with questions or concerns, she met with a terse answer. This did nothing to reassure her. Family, friends, and professionals did all they could to ease her fears, but to no avail.

One day during Eucharistic Adoration, she poured her heart out to Jesus. Spiritually, she was given the understanding that loving someone who doesn't love you back (as she thought was the case with Jay) is how our Lord loves us from the cross. She remembered how Jesus had told his disciples that it's easy to love those who love you, but we're called to do something far more difficult. We're called to love those who don't love us back. This profound revelation changed Bethany's heart.

"Throughout this whole ordeal, not only did I gain an understanding of how challenging it is to love like Christ—freely and without the consolation of that love being returned and even being outright rejected by your own child—but also how essential and beautiful that kind of love is," she wrote. "I learned to love Christ more; I learned to trust his power to heal in God's timing, not mine. Through the intercession of the Blessed Mother, I was led to understand the heart of Christ."

Jay graduated high school and attended the local university in the fall. He was still dark, sullen, and angry, but Bethany knew that Jay would have to work things out himself; all she could do was pray. When Jay came home for Christmas, Bethany's fretting began all over again. It seemed as if nothing had changed. One night, she sat in her family prayer corner thinking things over. She prayed and asked herself whether her worrying was doing any good for either herself or Jay. Then, the answer came. *Nothing. Nothing good was coming from the fear and worry. Nothing good would ever come from it.* And so Bethany released her fear to God. Suddenly, she felt completely free.

It required hope, patience, persistence, and love, but ever so slowly, Jay began to mature and find peace and meaning in life. His relationship with his mother healed and he began calling spontaneously just to tell her he loved her. Laughter, joking, warmth, friendliness, and his good-natured personality returned to him. He graduated college, moved to another state, and started a new life there—one that was free of the memories of the past and optimistic for a new, fruitful life.

Of her experiences, Bethany wrote, "In a culture that worships 'easy,' there's much more value in difficult. Remembering that has helped me heal, understand, and has confirmed once again how amazing, awesome, and wise our God is and how he's with us through it all, embracing all our pain and transforming it to joy. It doesn't matter if you fall; we all fall. It matters that you lift yourself up and walk, run, even dance, knowing you are never alone, confident that you are loved beyond comprehension. It matters that you trust that the works of God are all good, and that in its own time, every need is supplied. If just one person believes there is a God or is moved to a deeper understanding of his merciful love, if just one person seeks help earlier than I did for their child who is suicidal, I will not have written this in vain."

Bethany exchanged yokes with Jesus as she sat in her prayer corner. In her prayer that night, she concluded that trying to carry her solitary yoke was doing no good for herself or for her son. She hadn't accepted Jesus' yoke. She hadn't been pulling *with* Jesus; she'd been pulling *against* him. The result was chaos. Once she took on our Lord's yoke, her burden lightened and her soul found rest.

"Take my yoke upon you and learn from me, for I am meek and humble of heart; and you will find rest for yourselves."

Consider the burden you carry right now. Whose yoke are you using to carry it? Are you stubbornly clinging to your ruddy, solitary yoke? Or, have you allowed our Lord to place *his* yoke upon your shoulders? Jesus is inviting you to put your yoke down and take up his. He wants you to learn from him as you step forward and to take refuge in his gentle, lowly heart. He promised that, if you do that, you will find rest for your soul.

IN ME YOU HAVE PEACE

"I have told you this so that you might have peace in me. In the world you will have trouble, but take courage, I have conquered the world." JOHN 16:33

Every time I work on a book manuscript, strange things happen, almost as if "someone" was trying to deter me from getting my work done. When this happened with my first couple of books, I thought it was just my imagination. For example, once I sat down to work only to discover that the file for my manuscript was completely missing. I searched everywhere on my computer for it, but it was nowhere to be found. I had to resort to an older version of the manuscript, which meant recreating thousands of words. At least I had saved that older version! On another occasion, I had to reinstall some software because it had ceased to function for no apparent reason. Fights between the kids or their sudden mishaps, bumps, and bruises are part of normal family life, but they seemed to pop up at an accelerated rate when I was working on the book. Any of these things could be rationalized and discounted, and that's exactly what I did.

That's exactly what I did, that is, until I began the third book. My first two books speak about God's providence. But the third book really drew fire, so to speak. The book is about building strong Catholic families, and no one hates families more than the evil one himself. Not only did the "usual" things happen—equipment and software failures and random mishaps in and around the house—but during the writing of that book, we had serious illness in the family, one of which required hospitalization and a medical procedure—for me! By this time, I'd begun to suspect that something more was at work than technical failures, human error, and happenstance.

"Somebody" wasn't pleased with my work and wanted to distract me away from it!

Going into my fourth book, I was determined not to be caught off guard. I expected to get more of the same as I worked, especially since it's a book for mothers about looking to the Blessed Virgin Mary for example, inspiration, and intercession. I was right. It was same ol' same ol', with the addition of some new pranks. One day, I was home alone and with the house quiet and the phone ringer turned off, figuring I could get a ton of work done. I was busy working in the home office when I suddenly felt a heavy thud hit the side of the house on the outside. It was as if a heavy object of some kind had been lugged against the house. Concerned, I rose, checked the entire inside of the house and then walked around the whole outside of the house. I didn't find a single thing that could have caused that noise—no sign of damage, and no disturbance anywhere on our property or the adjacent properties. Weeks later, my daughter was in a car accident. She was fine, but the car was not—it had been totaled. There was a whole list of strange incidents that happened while working on that book.

This pattern worsened while I attempted to complete the fifth book manuscript. Illness, depression, discord, inexplicable incidents around the house, and crises of all sorts hit my family and me, including the feeling of oppression, doubt, and a tough case of writer's block, all of which made it truly hard to keep going on the book. Yet, I did keep going. Just as with my other books, I knew I'd been called by God to write that one, and I was not about to let anyone or anything come between me and following God's will. This manuscript has been no different. For all of them, it was tribulation after tribulation as I tried to follow God's promptings with my writing. I'm sure it will be the same way for the next manuscript too.

I tell you these things, not to scare you—you shouldn't be scared by them—but rather to encourage you in your own tribulations. Because of what happened during the first couple of manuscripts, I learned to arm myself against these happenings by hovering close to our Lord, surrendering myself to him and allowing his grace to be my shield. I relied on spiritual direction, received the sacraments often, and spent time in solitary prayer at home and before the monstrance in Eucharistic Adoration. I'd share what's on my mind and heart with our Lord, even venting a little (okay, I vented a lot), and asking for his blessings, encouragements, and protection. I also clung tightly to his dear Mother as my protector and intercessor. As our Catholic tradition tells us, Jesus "gave" Mary to us as he hung dying on the cross.

> Standing by the cross of Jesus were his mother and his mother's sister, Mary the wife of Clopas, and Mary of Magdala. When Jesus saw his mother and the disciple there whom he loved, he said to his mother, "Woman, behold, your son." Then he said to the disciple, "Behold, your mother." And from that hour the disciple took her into his home. After this, aware that everything was now finished, in order that the scripture might be fulfilled, Jesus said, "I thirst."
> ✳ *John 19:25–28*

When Jesus placed Mary into John's care and John into Mary's care, he was intending his words to include all humankind.

When those words were spoken, Mary's motherhood broadened to include John as her son physically and all of us as her sons and daughters spiritually. She truly became our heavenly Mother. On John's part, his agreement to take Mary into his home is practical in the physical sense but also symbolic for all people—we accept Christ, and so we accept his mother as well. With Mary to mother me during these tribulations, I felt secure in her motherly arms. You will feel that security and love, too, in your own tribulations if you turn to her.

Initially, of course, I was frightened by these strange occurrences. But that didn't last long because I saw them for what they were—a challenge and an urging to draw closer to Christ and believe more firmly in his promises. I don't know for a fact that all that took place during my work on the books was spiritual warfare, although I strongly suspect that most of it was. Some, however, could have been trials allowed by the heavenly Father for my sake as a way of strengthening me in my faith and perhaps preparing me for something that is yet to come in my life. What did our Lord say? *In the world you have tribulation.* Yes, indeed, the mere fact of being human and living on this earth means that our lives won't be perfect. But, Jesus also urges us to "be of good cheer." Why? Because he has overcome the world! So, no matter how tough or chaotic things got while I wrote my books, I didn't let it rattle me because I knew that all the tribulations I had to face— or will ever have to face—have been overcome by our Lord Jesus Christ. Whether it's the evil one trying to shake me from my mission or the heavenly Father asking from me the heroic hurdling of obstacles, I am confident that all will be well and

I can find peace in Christ. You too will find that peace in him if you allow him to step in and take over.

St. Augustine of Hippo suffered manifold tribulations. Sadly, he brought most of them on himself. Born in 354 AD in Tagaste, Augustine was raised Christian by his mother, St. Monica. His father, Patricius, was a pagan. When Augustine was just sixteen years old, he fell into bad company and engaged in "a succession of dark lusts," as he describes in his *Confessions*.[19] His promiscuity soon turned into sexual addiction. "Instead, I foamed in my wickedness, following the rushing of my own tides, leaving You and going beyond all Your laws," he wrote.[20] His ambitions took him to Carthage and then Milan, and things got worse from there. He was caught in a "cauldron of illicit loves," pursuing unclean desires and objects of his lust. He was plagued by suspicions, fears, temper fits, and quarrels. He was quite gifted and became a leader in the School of Rhetoric. Unfortunately, he strayed into the heresy of Manicheism, took on a mistress, and had a son with her. All the while, he had not only turned from God but mocked those who followed Christ. Suffice it to say that, in his early years, St. Augustine was not a very wholesome guy!

When he was thirty-two years old, Augustine suffered a debilitating respiratory illness that required a respite from teaching. Through the prayers and influence of his mother, St. Augustine was introduced to St. Ambrose, bishop of Milan. Ambrose awakened in Augustine a yearning to know more

---

19 *Confessions*, Augustine of Hippo, transl. F.J. Sheed, Second ed., ©2006, Hackett Publishing Company, Book II, I, p. 25.

20 Ibid., p. 26.

about Christianity. One day, while reclining in the garden, Augustine heard a child's voice singing, "Take up and read. Take up and read."[21] At first, he thought there was a child in the garden playing a game with him. But then he realized that it was a message from God to open and read the Scriptures; so he located a Bible. He took it up, opened it randomly, and read the first passage that met his eyes. It was from St. Paul's Letter to the Romans.

> let us conduct ourselves properly as in the day, not in orgies and drunkenness, not in promiscuity and licentiousness, not in rivalry and jealousy. But put on the Lord Jesus Christ, and make no provision for the desires of the flesh.
> ✳ *Romans 13:13–14*

God—first through the child's voice and then through the Scriptures—revealed to Augustine the gravity of his wayward life. That moment was the beginning of Augustine's turning away from his sinful ways and toward God. After his conversion, Augustine was baptized, ordained a priest and later a bishop, founded monasteries, and became a famous Catholic writer and Doctor of the Church. He spent the rest of his life passionately serving Christ and his church. This is the same man who once was addicted to sex and debauchery!

St. Augustine's poor early life choices brought upon him countless tribulations. All the while, St. Monica remained both physically and spiritually close to her son, begging God's mercy for him and praying untiringly for his conversion. For

---

21 Ibid, p. 76.

decades, he resisted until finally God's grace broke through his hardened heart. Despite his self-inflicted tribulations, there was reason for hope. In Jesus, Augustine found peace, because he has overcome the world.

We all face tribulations of one kind or another. For many of us, those tribulations are caused by other people in our lives or unfortunate situations that are out of our control. Perhaps you've been cheated in a business deal, betrayed by a close friend, or involved in a serious car accident. Maybe you've fallen into ill health or were born with a chronic disease or disability. You might be involved in a relationship that suddenly has become abusive or are caught in family turmoil. These are tribulations caused by someone else's choices. Some of us, however, bring on our tribulations by the choices we ourselves have made. Sexual promiscuity, dishonesty, gambling, drug or alcohol abuse, cohabitating, crime, adultery, and recklessness, for example, are all behaviors we choose that will surely lead to tribulations. Like St. Augustine, we're the cause of our own woes.

Regardless of how our tribulations came to be, we have every reason to be of good cheer. No matter what the trouble is, God is more powerful. No matter how difficult things might be, we can find peace in our Lord. From the worst sin to the most horrendous calamity, Jesus has overcome it because he has overcome the world. That is his promise to us.

Jerome[22] is a church pastor and former seminary instructor. His story is one of tribulations brought on by bad choices made by his daughter. It's an especially helpful story, I think,

---

22 Not his real name.

because it shows that tribulations of this kind can touch any-one's family—even the family of a church pastor with a doctor-ate in theology. It's also a story of Jesus' promise to be of good cheer no matter what, because he has overcome the world.

JEROME: THE WORST NEWS EVER

The call from Jerome's son started out ominously, "Mom and Dad, are you sitting down? Sophia[23] is using heroin," he said. Jerome and his wife were mentally and emotionally shocked. They were devastated, depressed, fearful for her life, guilt-stricken, and filled with questions about their parenting skills. A myriad of questions raced through their minds. *How could such a thing happen? Our wonderful daughter had fallen into the world of heroin without our knowing it. What signals had we missed? How could we have been so blind? How had she been so successful in lying to us?* They went numb, almost as if their emotional systems had involuntarily shut down.

But they had no time for themselves; they had to spring into action. They lived in the Southwest and Sophia lived in the West, but they didn't know her exact location. After several calls, they learned she was in Mexico. They had no idea if she was in prison or even alive for that matter. God seemed remote in this terrible situation. Jerome prayed what he describes as a very selfish prayer, "God I have given you my life for ministry. How could you let this happen to me?" He wasn't thinking of his daughter; he was only thinking of himself. To make matters worse, the day their son called with

---

23 Not her real name.

the bad news was Jerome's first Sunday as pastor of his new church. This certainly added to the stress.

Through a great deal of hurried detective work, Jerome and his wife learned the next day that Sophia was returning to her home Monday night. They went there, made arrangements for her at a detox center, and waited. When she returned home, they walked in unannounced and said, "We know you have been using heroin. We want you to come to get help." Her response was twofold: "Okay. But I will not go cold-turkey, because I've tried to quit ten times and thought I was going to die each time." They later discovered that she had cried out to God many times for help. Her purse was full of cards with Bible verses related to God's protection and deliverance.

Sophia went to detox and by Thursday was declared ready for treatment. She chose to relocate to her parents' city and to the same hospital where Jerome's brother had been chief of staff of cardiology. When she checked in, they were asked by a number of people if she was related. That was an initial embarrassment because of his prominence in the hospital; but they soon got over it, because they realized that Sophia's treatment and sobriety were far more important than any negative thoughts people might have had. Sophia's life was more important than their reputation.

The next morning after checking her into the treatment center and with desolate feelings of depression, fear, and loneliness, Jerome and his wife attended a Nar-Anon meeting—a support group for people whose loved ones use drugs. Jerome thought to himself, "What in the world am I doing here? I am a pastor. I do not *need* help. I *give* help." But, he realized, he did need help. He needed to be quiet and humble and listen to what the others had to say. As he listened to their stories, he got to know them as a group of people who were all committed to getting or staying healthy, to supporting one another, and to helping each participant know that the addict is responsible for his or her own sobriety. It was an important group to be in.

The recovering addicts in the church overwhelmed Jerome and his wife with love and support. They were deeply impressed by them, and through their help they came to understand that it is what we keep in secret that keeps us from getting well. That is one of the great pieces of wisdom for the parents and loved ones of addicts—they need other people. Jerome reflected on St. Paul's Letter to the Romans, "Rejoice with those who rejoice; mourn with those who mourn."[24] and his Letter to the Galatians, "Carry each other's burdens, and in this way you will fulfill the law of Christ."[25] In their crisis, Jerome and his wife learned that they couldn't walk the road alone. They needed people who could weep with them and help carry their burdens from time to time. They have no idea what they would have done without the help and support of the Nar-Anon group.

Sophia finished rehabilitation and has been clean and sober for many years. She has finished her bachelor's and master's degrees and is now an addiction counselor at a Salvation Army treatment center in the Southwest. She attends Alcoholics Anonymous meetings regularly and knows that sobriety is one day at a time; it is a daily walk of faith. Jerome's family doesn't hide the fact that Sophia is a recovering addict, and

---

24 NIV Romans 12:15.

25 NIV Galatians 6:2.

they've come to understand that they are not to be blamed for Sophia's mistakes. After her release from rehab, she told her parents, "You taught me the right way. I made the wrong decisions."

About the ordeal, Jerome cites St. Paul's Second Letter to the Corinthians, "who comforts us in all our troubles, so that we can comfort those in any trouble with the comfort we ourselves receive from God."[26] For this reason, he and his wife started a ministry to help pastors, missionaries, and Christian workers whose kids abuse drugs and/or alcohol. Jerome also has written a book for parents of children abusing drugs or alcohol.

Looking back on the crisis with Sophia, Jerome wrote, "One of the most important things I have learned in this process is that God is always near…even when we think he is not. The Apostle Paul's words in his Letter to the Romans have become a great help to me in praying when I feel desperate and do not even know what to say or think: 'In the same way, the Spirit helps us in our weakness. We do not know what we ought to pray for, but the Spirit himself intercedes for us through wordless groans. And he who searches our hearts knows the mind of the Spirit, because the Spirit intercedes for God's people in accordance with the will of God.'[27]

"It is also comforting to know that God does not expect perfection from us," Jerome continued. "Instead, he understands that we will have bad days. I think this is why the Apostle Peter is so honest and helpful when he writes, 'Cast

---

26 NIV 2 Corinthians 1:4.

27 NIV Romans 8:26–27.

all your anxiety on him because he cares for you.'[28] Peter did not say that once we become Christ-followers we will never again have issues or concerns. Rather, he wrote that when we are anxious we can cast those anxieties on him. That is a great comfort to me."

After his conversion, St. Augustine came to see this life in a different way. It wasn't until he got to know God better that he discovered the real object of his heart's desire—God. He expresses this beautifully in his *Confessions*.

> Thou dost so excite him that to praise Thee is his joy. For thou hast made us for Thyself and our hearts are restless until they rest in Thee. Grant me, O Lord, to know which is the soul's first movement toward Thee—to implore Thy aid or to utter its praise of Thee; and whether it must know Thee before it can implore. For it would seem clear that no one can call on Thee without first knowing Thee for if he did he might invoke another than Thee, knowing Thee not.[29]

Our hearts are indeed restless until they rest in God. St. Augustine's point is valid. Without knowing God, we'll be

28　NIV 1 Peter 5:7.

29　*Confessions*, p. 3.

tempted to invoke someone or something other than God. For example, consider what it's like to try to rid yourself of a bad habit—overeating, perhaps. It may not seem like a tribulation, but for lots of people, it can be a behavior that causes hardship. You could try to power through it, resisting every urge on your own volition. You could try different things like limiting portions and the kinds of food you keep in the house. That would help, but it doesn't get to the core of the problem. For most people, overeating is a matter of eating to satisfy emotions rather than the body. And why would you be trying to satisfy your emotions with food? Likely because you're not satisfying them with God. You need that "high" but are looking for it in the wrong place. God is the ultimate source of all your strength and he is interested in every aspect of your well-being.

Whether the tribulation is seemingly minor, like overeating, or drastic and dangerous, like substance abuse and addiction, God is interested. He wants to be your strength and will give you the grace you need to face not only the one tribulation that weighs you down right now but all the tribulations in your life, past, present, and future. Jesus became man and lived on this earth so that he could experience tribulation just as we do. In fact, the tribulations he faced are far worse than any we might face. He wants us to rely on him, to trust him, and to find peace in him despite the chaos or calamities around us, our sinfulness, and the doubts or fears we harbor in our hearts. He promises that we definitely will have tribulations. More important, he promises us that he already has overcome them for us.

THE HOLY SPIRIT WILL TEACH YOU

"When they take you before synagogues and before rulers and authorities, do not worry about how or what your defense will be or about what you are to say. For the holy Spirit will teach you at that moment what you should say." LUKE 12:11–12

When I meditate on this Scripture passage, I'm reminded of two heroic women from the Old Testament who desperately needed the Holy Spirit to tell them what to say in a dire situation. Those two heroines are Esther and Susanna.

The entire Book of Esther is exciting, with twists and turns and surprises. What strikes me most, however, is the way Esther relied on the Spirit for guidance in her urgent quest to save her people from destruction. Esther, although Jewish, was the wife of King Ahasuerus. All was well until one day when Esther's father, Mordecai, refused to honor one of the king's henchmen named Haman. A devout Jew, Mordecai had pledged only to honor God, so giving Haman the honor he demanded would violate Mordecai's faith. This so angered Haman that he goaded the king into ordering the annihilation of the entire Jewish people. Sadly, King Ahasuerus agreed.

When Mordecai found out about the king's decree, he sought help from Queen Esther. She said to him, "All the servants of the king and the people of his provinces know that any man or woman who goes to the king in the inner court without being summoned is subject to the same law—death. Only if the king extends the golden scepter will such a person live. Now as for me, I have not been summoned to the king for thirty days" (Esther 4:11).

Approaching the king without first being called by him could mean a death sentence for Esther. Knowing this and at the same time knowing the plight of the Jews, Mordecai gave Esther a classic response that has often been quoted throughout history. "Who knows—perhaps it was for a time such as this that you became queen?" (Esther 4:14).

In a sense, Mordecai had cornered Esther. Who but she, with her unique position as queen and Jew, could better advocate for the Israelites' cause? And so Esther agreed to Mordecai's request. She instructed him to have the Jews fast for three days, and she and her maids would fast as well. At the end of the three days, she would approach the king.

On the fourth day, Esther put on her royal garments and stood in the courtyard outside the king's audience chamber. He noticed her there and, because of her beauty and charm, favored her. As was the custom, King Ahasuerus extended his golden scepter to her and she touched it before speaking. Then, she invited him to a banquet she had prepared, and he accepted. During the banquet, he promised to grant her request even if it meant half his kingdom. Her request was that he come to another banquet the next day. In the meantime, Haman spitefully requested from the king that Mordecai should be put to death by impalement the next day instead of on the day assigned for the Jews' destruction. Haman would have gotten his way had the king not made an important discovery that night: Mordecai had saved the king's life by exposing two of his guards as would-be assassins. For this, King Ahasuerus granted Mordecai great honor.

The next day at the banquet, Esther pleaded for the lives of herself and her people.

She begged, "If I have found favor with you, O king, and if it pleases your majesty, I ask that my life be spared, and I beg that you spare the lives of my people. For we have been sold, I and my people, to be destroyed, killed, and annihilated. If we were only to be sold into slavery I would remain silent, for then our distress would not have been worth troubling the king" (Esther 7:3).

King Ahasuerus granted Esther's bold request, and the lives of the Jews were spared.

Like Esther, Susanna faced a death sentence. For Susanna, however, the death sentence came as the result of false accusations.

Susanna was the wife of a wealthy man named Joakim. She was a beautiful, virtuous, and God-fearing woman dedicated to her husband and to her faith. Joakim owned a lovely garden where Susanna liked to walk while her husband, a man of great import, met with elders and judges on matters of concern. Two of the elders became enamored with Susanna, and lust for her grew in their wicked hearts. One day, they decided to satisfy their lust by trying to force Susanna to give in to their lustful desires.

On that day, the elders had been hiding in the garden spying on her. Also on that day, Susanna chose to bathe in the garden's pool. When she sent her maids into the house to fetch oil and soap for her bath, the elders approached her. If she didn't remain silent and give in to them, they threatened, they'd make up a lie about her, saying that they'd caught her having an affair with a young man in the garden. Because it would be against God's law, Susanna refused the men's request and instead screamed for help. When help came, the elders proceeded with their evil lie and pretended that they had just caught Susanna and a young man in the throes of an affair, but that the young man had fought them off and escaped. A bogus trial was immediately set up and Susanna was brought before the judges, facing the death sentence. As if that wasn't enough, the elders further shamed Susanna by insisting that she be unveiled before the crowd that had gathered. Poor Susanna! It was her word against the words of the two elders. She had no one to defend her—even Joakim had been confused by the elders' testimony—and no way to explain herself. It seemed that she was doomed.

Still, she didn't give up. She turned to God in her distress and called upon the Holy Spirit for guidance. She cried out, "Eternal God, you know what is hidden and are aware of all things before they come to be: you know that they have testified falsely against me. Here I am about to die, though I have done none of the things for which these men have condemned me" (Daniel 13:42–43).

Her prayers were not in vain. Standing in the crowd was a young boy named Daniel. As he observed the scene playing out before him, he was suddenly "stirred up" by the Holy Spirit and prompted to help Susanna. With wisdom beyond his years given him by the Spirit, Daniel devised a clever plot to catch the elders in their lie. By questioning them separately, he uncovered discrepancies in their stories and proved Susanna's innocence. Thus, she was saved from death—and from shame.

These two examples are extremely useful to me because they show two very different ways of living out our Lord's promise to send the Holy Spirit when we're defenseless in a serious situation. In Esther's case, she was prompted by the Spirit to beg for the lives of herself and her people. Courageously and confidently, she did the speaking. In Susanna's case, she prayed for help and then allowed someone else—Daniel—to speak in her defense. Both dilemmas began with a prayer for guidance, took two different routes, but then ended up with the same solution. The Holy Spirit put the right words in the right mouth at the right time and saved the day.

There have been so many times like these in my own life that I simply can't count them all. Either I'm in a tight spot or someone close to me is, and the Holy Spirit intervenes and gives the right words to the right people. Sometimes I speak on my own behalf, and sometimes someone else speaks for me. Either way, it's the Spirit who saves the day. I can think of one situation in particular where the Spirit prompted me in what *not* to say rather than what *to* say.

Many years ago, I was enlisted to help with a ministry for young women. Odd circumstances saw to it that I suddenly was made the one responsible for it rather than just helping with it. Soon I found myself caught in the middle of conflicting personalities and directives from the people I reported to, and the ministry became a mess. It came to a head at a meeting during which all fingers were pointed at me. Not one other person there was willing to own up to the parts he or she had played in making the mess. In my mind and heart, I uttered a pleading prayer to the Holy Spirit for guidance. In that moment, the Spirit made clear to me that I should remain silent rather than try to speak in my own defense. At that point, anything I had to say would only make things worse.

So, I listened to what everyone had to say, and when they were all finished I politely excused myself from the meeting and left. Hurt and frustrated, I allowed myself to have a good long cry on the way home. And, I suspect a couple of dings to my reputation have resulted from it. Still, I felt assured that all went according to God's will because I'd followed the promptings of the Holy Spirit.

During that meeting and in many other difficult moments in my life, our Lord kept his promise: *"Do not worry about how or what your defense will be or about what you are to say. For the holy Spirit will teach you at that moment what you should say."*

Barbara Stoefen has a similar story to tell about the promptings of the Holy Spirit in a difficult situation. When her daughter became addicted to drugs, she longed for the right thing to do or the perfect thing to say. Her mother's instinct urged her to take action, but the Holy Spirit urged her to "let go."

BARBARA STOEFEN: CHOOSE JOY

Barbara and her husband were married in 1980, had two children, a boy and a girl, and lived in the Northwest. By most people's standards, they were the average American family. Barbara tells people that they were the proverbial "Cleavers" from the 1950s sitcom *Leave It to Beaver.* They were committed, involved parents and raised their children in the faith. Barbara thought that would give them certain assurances, and she believed that there was no way addiction ever could touch her family. Little did she know addiction is a brain disease that can affect absolutely anyone.

Barbara's daughter, Tiffany,[30] was a happy, fun-loving child, albeit a very sensitive one. She was extremely bright and had good friends and a loving family. But she was shy and unsure of herself, and she could sometimes be withdrawn. When she was eleven years old, the death of her grandfather triggered a depressive episode. At the time, Barbara wasn't aware that depression is one of the major risk factors for addiction. Tiffany didn't party in high school and didn't have her first drink until after graduation. The alcohol seemed to fix the discomfort she felt inside, and she was soon using it to manage her life. When she had an emotional collapse her first semester of college, she admitted to Barbara that alcohol had become a problem for her. That realization, however, didn't curb her drinking.

Over a period of a few years, Tiffany's drinking escalated, and other drugs were added to the picture. Most of this was not apparent to the family. They knew only that her life looked muddled. Daily marijuana use became the norm, and Barbara knew she'd tried cocaine once in college. She did everything a mother could do to steer her daughter away from it all, but the concept of addiction never occurred to her. She simply assumed Tiffany was making bad choices.

Between the ages of eighteen and twenty-two, Tiffany's life was embroiled in chaos. She was in and out of college and in and out of multiple relationships with boys, and she moved frequently. Life was messy, and there seemed to be one crisis after another. After a move to the Southwest and Barbara's rescue mission to bring her home, things really unraveled.

---

30 Not her real name.

She was different. The once-loving Tiffany was now agitated all of the time and very disrespectful of her family. They finally asked her to find another place to live. That moment was one of the worst days of Barbara's life.

Months later, on Easter morning, Tiffany arrived for a family gathering and confided in Barbara that she was using meth, and "she was happier than she'd ever been." Barbara knew, on the other hand, that life had just changed forever.

What followed was about eighteen months of hell. Tiffany's life completely fell apart. She soon became a daily meth user and was no longer in school. She lost her job, lost her place to live, and was couch surfing in the homes of strangers. She took on a skeletal appearance and was quickly looking like the drug addict and homeless person she'd become. The family rarely saw her and had virtually no relationship with her.

Then the legal consequences began. In order to find drugs to feed a growing habit, Tiffany was lying, cheating, stealing, getting arrested, and going to jail. Barbara sometimes wondered if losing her daughter in this way might be worse than death. She had lost the very essence of who Tiffany was because she had become someone else. It felt like such a profound waste that Barbara didn't know how she'd find a way to live with the sadness and the grief. The few times Barbara did see her, or when she called from jail with raging demands to be bailed out, she just kept losing Tiffany over and over again.

Barbara used to go into the garage and rage and scream and cry at God—rage that God had allowed this to happen. How was she to find relief? What was she supposed to do? After several weeks of this, God answered her. She heard an answer rise from within, and it was this: "Give her to me."

That moment changed Barbara forever. She turned her precious girl over to God, because he'd said so. She didn't know what the outcome would be, but she knew whatever it was, it would not be up to her.

About this, Barbara wrote, "I didn't hang on. I let go. It is completely counterintuitive for a parent, but we truly have no power over the choices of another person...not even a person we raised. So, I gave my daughter to God and trusted him with whatever was to be. I truly had to be at the end of myself in order to do this. I continued to do some practical things, and advocated for my daughter whenever I could, but I let go of trying to control the situation or to force the outcome. Trying to control a situation that can't be controlled will only make us sick."

Barbara realized just how much she had been changed in that moment while attending her son's last basketball game his senior year of high school. Unexpectedly, she noticed her heart soaring, and she was having the time of her life. Her son was playing his best game of his high school career, and it was thrilling to watch. On the other side of town, Tiffany sat in a jail cell. Barbara marveled at how God had allowed her to feel such joy in the presence of such sadness. She concluded that it was a matter of choice—she chose to feel joy. She felt God close to her, protecting her heart and mind.

Choosing joy was part of the recovery process for Barbara, but also for Tiffany. During that time, Barbara focused on what she could change in herself that could improve the situation and heal her family. The best way she could help Tiffany was to continue loving her, refrain from judging her, and not shame her while at the same time working to become the best person she could possibly be. She wanted the family home to be a place to which Tiffany would want to return and not a place of judgment and conflict. And, Barbara made it clear to Tiffany that she would survive even if Tiffany did not.

Eventually, Tiffany took a step toward change and asked for help. The family had a plan for this should the moment ever come, and they were able to send Tiffany away for several months of treatment. With help, time, commitment, and a willingness to replace drug use with positive coping tools, Tiffany found recovery. She's remained alcohol and drug free for more than twelve years.

Tiffany's addiction and recovery have taught Barbara many things, and she uses what she's learned to help other families with members suffering addiction. She's written and spoken publicly about addiction and leads a support group in her community. For Barbara, sorrow turned to joy at the first realization that God was there with her throughout. She's never been closer to him than during that time, and the epiphany she'd received that amazing day showed her that she has a special purpose in life. In that moment, she'd given herself permission to carry on and to find joy wherever she could. She refers to Victor Frankl's book *Man's Search for Meaning* as her inspiration. "It helps me to know there is a Power in the world that is greater than myself, One that is capable of achieving what I cannot," she wrote. "This gives me hope. I can choose joy; I can choose an attitude, despite life circumstances that may be out of my control."

Man's Search for Meaning is a timeless work with a profound message about suffering, purpose, and the meaning of life. In it, Frankl, a noted psychiatrist, relays his experiences in the Auschwitz concentration camp during World War II and the insights he gained from his time there. "For the meaning of life differs from man to man, from day to day and from hour to hour," he wrote. "What matters, therefore, is not the meaning of life in general but the meaning of a person's life at a given moment."[31]

Regarding suffering, he wrote, "There are situations in which one is cut off from the opportunity to do one's work or to enjoy one's life; but what never can be ruled out is the unavoidability of suffering. In accepting this challenge to suffer bravely, life has a meaning up to the last moment, and it retains this meaning literally to the end. In other words, life's meaning is an unconditional one for it even includes the potential meaning of suffering."[32]

These statements are true for you and for every stage of your life. In choosing to suffer bravely, you give substance and meaning to your suffering. You can choose to cower in the corner and let havoc rule or, like Esther, you can dare to plead your case and save yourself and others. You can give in to hopelessness or, like Susanna, you can stand strong, confident

---

31 *Man's Search for Meaning*, by Viktor E. Frankl, trans. Ilse Lasch, ©1959, Beacon Press, p. 110.

32 Ibid., p. 116.

in God's wisdom and ability to reveal the truth even in the darkest hour. You can refute God's grace and continue struggling or, like Barbara Stoefen, you can choose joy and let go so that God can take control. You can—joyfully—choose to believe Jesus' promise that the Holy Spirit will teach you what you need to do and say in that critical hour.

Promise Nine

All things are possible *with* God

Jesus looked at them and said,
"For human beings it is impossible,
but not for God. All things are possible
for God." MARK 10:27

W hen we miscarried our second child, I was devastated. It was a long, drawn out miscarriage, which extended the agony. To make matters worse, the miscarriage didn't fully resolve, and I had to be hospitalized days later to undergo a procedure to clear the womb and protect me from serious infection. When we buried our baby, I felt as though I'd buried myself. Even before I learned I was pregnant, I dreamed that I was going to have a baby girl. I even dreamed what she'd look like, down to the tiniest detail. That dream was so real to me that, when we discovered that I actually *was* pregnant, my husband and I immediately named the child Elizabeth.

Our first pregnancy had been a tough one, but with God's grace we made it through. Our baby boy was born prematurely, yet he was strong and thrived with excellent care in the neonatal intensive care unit. After all that, I was a bit nervous about getting pregnant again. But my specialist assured us that it was unlikely that the same problems would occur again. We wanted children so badly that we decided—admittedly a bit nervously—to trust in God and open ourselves to another pregnancy. Then, I miscarried. I felt like my body had betrayed not only my husband and me, but also our innocent little Elizabeth. For months, I couldn't stand being around babies, especially babies with dark hair, as I'd dreamed our baby would have. I'd burst into tears every time I heard a baby cry. When Elizabeth died inside of me, I was certain I'd never feel joy again.

People can say some very hurtful things when you miscarry. They don't mean to be hurtful, but it affects you that way. The most common remark I heard was, "Oh, don't worry. You'll have another baby." I didn't want *another* baby; I wanted the baby I'd lost. No child could, or ever has, replaced Elizabeth. And with my health history, I wasn't sure it was even possible for me to have another baby. Back then, it seemed impossible that we would ever have the family for which we longed.

Indeed, it *was* impossible, if we looked at it from a strictly human perspective. I was sure I knew what my body was—or wasn't—capable of doing. I wasn't prayerfully considering what God could do with and through my body. Within a year after miscarrying Elizabeth, and with my doctor's encouragement, I was pregnant again. We gave birth to a beautiful baby girl. Admittedly, that too was a difficult pregnancy; she was born four weeks early; and a few days after birth she contracted a systemic staph infection and we nearly lost her. Three years later, our second son was born after a healthy, event-free pregnancy. Five years later, our fourth child—a boy—was born ten weeks prematurely and seriously sick. It took him until the age of five, but he finally recovered and regained his strength. Yes, there were ups and downs through each of the pregnancies. But it's those same ups and downs that helped my husband and me grow as a couple and all of us grow as a family. It was never about what my body could or could not do, but rather what God could do through us.

Today, all four of my living children are amazing, capable individuals who are following their own dreams and starting their own families. Although I've never stopped missing Elizabeth, the emptiness has been filled by God's love and mercy and the knowledge that our family has a personal advocate ceaselessly interceding for us in heaven. Despite not being able to see or hold her, I feel her presence close to me always. As if this wasn't enough, God gave us an extra special gift in addition to all of this. Many years after our miscarriage, my brother-in-law and his wife gave birth to their second child—a girl—and asked us to be godparents They named her Elizabeth, after St. Elizabeth Ann Seton, just as we'd named our own Elizabeth. We haven't had the joy of watching our own Elizabeth grow and excel, but we have had the joy of watching our goddaughter Elizabeth grow and excel. God is good!

Barry Adkin also knows what it's like to lose a child. He lost his eighteen-year-old son, Kevin, to alcohol poisoning. Understandably, it was a tragic event that devastated Barry, but only for a time. With God's grace, Barry turned a tragedy into something very, very good. His story is incredible, and through it, I'm sure you'll see that with God all things are possible. With Barry's permission, I've used his real name so that readers may benefit from his wonderful ministry.

BARRY ADKIN: THE STILL SMALL VOICE

The awful knock on the door came on a Sunday morning—the day after Kevin Adkins' eighteenth birthday. Barry opened the door and learned from the sheriff standing there that his son had died the night before of alcohol poisoning. He'd been binge drinking to celebrate his birthday. The day that was supposed to mark the beginning of Kevin's adult life turned out to be his last.

The house had a reputation for being a party house, and Kevin knew a couple of the young men who lived there. They offered to let Kevin move in, and he accepted because it would be less expensive to rent a room there than renting an apartment. One of the roommates was twenty-eight years old and should have known better than to allow his younger and less experienced friends to binge drink. Police had been there on occasions in the past because there'd been trouble. Barry knew this and had had reservations about Kevin moving in there, but Barry knew he couldn't legally stop him since he was legally an adult. Friends suggested that Barry sue the municipality in which the house was located, but, what did it matter? No amount of money in the world would change the fact that Kevin was dead.

Barry's faith hadn't been particularly strong before, and Kevin's death certainly didn't help. He knew who God was, prayed, and went to church, but his was not a compelling faith. He especially struggled with the Lord's Prayer. There was a phrase in it that he never really understood, "Thy kingdom come; Thy will be done." He knew it in his head, but he hadn't taken it into his heart. He thought he was in control and didn't understand why God hadn't taken him instead of Kevin. He was angry about it; he was angry at God. He felt guilty about Kevin's death and kept asking himself what he could have done to stop it from happening. As a parent, he saw his number one job as keeping his children alive—everything else pales compared to that; Barry hadn't gotten the job done with Kevin. More than anything, he wished God would take him and let Kevin live. He refused to accept in his heart that God was in charge and that it wasn't for him to decide who would live and who would die.

There was a memorial for Kevin—he later would be cremated—with a viewing. Barry wouldn't go into the viewing room. He wanted to remember his son as he had lived and didn't want the memory of having seen him in the casket.

After the funeral, Barry was disengaged mentally and spiritually. Going to pick up Kevin's ashes after the cremation was incredibly difficult. Of that moment, he said, "You walk into the funeral home and they're playing nice music and you sit there in a comfortable chair at a big desk. The funeral director walks in and sets an urn in from of you. And that's all that's left of your kid. All that's left is what's inside of that urn."

Barry knew that couldn't possibly be all that was left of Kevin; there had to be more—Barry somehow had to make something good come from Kevin's death. In his pondering, he was reminded of Kevin's favorite movie, *Lonesome Dove*, with Robert Duvall and Tommy Lee Jones. The Western-genre miniseries is about two former Texas rangers who together run a livery in the small Texas border town of Lonesome Dove. At the end of the series, one of the rangers died on a cattle drive to Montana, but before he died, he made his partner promise to take him back to his Texas home—where he'd been happiest—to bury him. Barry had grown up in Montana and Kevin had been with him to visit there several times. He spoke often of wanting to move to Montana someday and buy a ranch. Barry decided to create his own version of *Lonesome Dove* for Kevin by taking his ashes to Montana—the place he'd dreamed of living someday—for burial.

"In the movie, it had been on horseback," Barry said. "So, I decided to walk because I couldn't do it on horseback."

With Kevin's ashes carefully stored in his backpack, Barry set out on the 1400-mile trek from Arizona to Montana, sticking to the side roads as he went. He had four months to complete his journey and plotted the distances and locations for each day. He stopped to speak to people he met along the way about Kevin and the dangers of alcohol poisoning. Often, he'd be asked to give a presentation to church or school groups. Barry's mission became known as "Kevin's Last Walk" and gained media attention as he went. The last three miles of the walk became its official finish and included speeches from Barry and other speakers, refreshments, and a private ceremony. Kevin's ashes were laid to rest on a plot of land owned by Barry. Having brought Kevin "home," Barry felt both relieved and sad. He was relieved at having made the journey successfully, but sad at the realization that it had indeed been Kevin's last walk.

Yet the walk had changed Barry. As he walked those solitary miles—mostly in silence—he slowly came to grips with the tragedy of Kevin's death and the effect it had had on him. On the path, what he described as a "still small voice" spoke to him in the quiet of his heart, and he at last was able to forgive himself and accept the fact that he really is not in charge— God is. Finally, he understood what those words, "thy will be done" meant. A new Barry was born, so to speak, and his faith moved from his head to his heart. He knew he could trust God to take care of everything. Part of Barry's life was gone, but a new one had opened up to him. In that, he found joy.

"God's got a plan and as they say, you do everything you can do and then you let God do what only he can do," Barry said.

Since completing the walk, Barry has been invited to collaborate with Mothers Against Drunk Driving (MADD)[33] and

---

33 Mothers Against Drunk Driving, http://www.madd.org/.

another organization called Not My Kid,[34] acting as spokesperson. He's continued his speaking ministry and authored a book titled, *Kevin's Last Walk: A Father's Final Journey with His Son*,[35] that chronicles Kevin's death and Barry's incredible journey. It has been in this—making something good come from something bad—that Barry's sorrow turned to joy.

All things are possible for God. Our Lord spoke those words in the context of the parable of the rich man who asked what he must do to enter the kingdom of heaven. When Jesus instructed him that he must give away all his riches and follow him, the rich man walked away sad because he realized he could never let go of his wealth. The disciples, astonished, asked Jesus how anyone could be saved when the standard is so high. Jesus replied, *"For human beings it is impossible, but not for God. All things are possible for God."*

Perhaps you can imagine letting go of material wealth if God asked you. Living simply can't be all that bad, can it? But what if God asked you to let go of wealth of another kind? What if it meant losing your health or reputation? What if it meant an unfavorable change in circumstances or the demise of a relationship? What if it meant the death of a loved one?

---

34 Not My Kid, https://notmykid.org/.

35 *Kevin's Last Walk: A Father's Final Journey with His Son*, Barry Adkins, Red Willow Publishing, 2011.

Would you walk away sad, or would you say "yes" to God's will? It might seem completely impossible to accept something so seemingly harsh.

Recall what happened to the prophet Elijah. He had tried and tried to convince the Israelites to turn away from their wicked ways and toward God. Not only did they refuse to listen to him, but they turned against God, killed all the other prophets, and hunted Elijah so they could kill him too. Elijah fled to Horeb, hiding from the Israelites in a cave. He no longer wanted to be God's messenger; he just wanted to be left alone. (see 1 Kings 19:11–21).

However, that's not what God wanted of him, and so, as Elijah hid there, God approached him and said, "Go out and stand on the mountain before the Lord; the Lord will pass by."

Elijah did as he was told. As he stood there a wind arose so forcefully that it split mountains and broke rocks into pieces. Despite its power, Elijah didn't experience God in the wind. After that there was an earthquake, but Elijah did not find God in that, either. Then there was fire, but again, Elijah did not sense God in it. Finally, there was sheer silence. In that silence, God spoke to Elijah, comforted him, and gave him directions to anoint a new king over Israel. Furthermore, he directed him to anoint a young man named Elisha who would become his servant and later take his place as prophet after Elijah was taken up into heaven.

You could be like Barry Adkins or the prophet Elijah, if you allowed God's still small voice to speak to you in the silence of your heart. He will never ask anything of you without walking beside you and providing you with grace to sustain you. There is no such thing as a life free from suffering, even for our Lord

Jesus. During his life on earth he suffered poverty, hardship, ridicule, sorrow, imprisonment, torture, and crucifixion. He gave everything for your sake and won't ask anything of you that will not somehow work out for the better even if it seems impossible at the time. That's because with God, all things are possible.

YOUR HEARTS WILL REJOICE

Jesus knew that they wanted to ask him, so he said to them, "Are you discussing with one another what I said, 'A little while and you will not see me, and again a little while and you will see me'? Amen, amen, I say to you, you will weep and mourn, while the world rejoices; you will grieve, but your grief will become joy. When a woman is in labor, she is in anguish because her hour has arrived; but when she has given birth to a child, she no longer remembers the pain because of her joy that a child has been born into the world. So you also are now in anguish. But I will see you again, and your hearts will rejoice, and no one will take your joy away from you." JOHN 16:19-22

Rod and Maria Dunlap were married in May 2011. In November of that year, they discovered that Maria was pregnant with their first child, and they were delighted beyond compare. At their twenty-week ultrasound in March 2012, they discovered that they were having a girl, adding to their excitement. They also discovered that their baby girl was in serious trouble—she had hypoplastic left heart syndrome, a condition in which the left side of the heart isn't properly formed and is incapable of functioning correctly. On that day, their lives changed forever.

ROD AND MARIA DUNLAP: EVERY LIFE HAS PURPOSE

After receiving the diagnosis, they left the appointment and sat in their car, crying. Eventually, they went home and tried to process and work through what the rest of the pregnancy and their future would be like.

"During that day, we prayed and worked through a lot going on inside of us," Rod said. "But by the end of the day, even though we still were confused, we realized that there was purpose here. Her life and ours now had a new and different meaning to them. God was leading us down a road that we would not have chosen to go, but one that he wanted us to go for his greater purpose. By the end of the day, we realized it was time to lace up our boot straps and get after it. And we did."

Despite the diagnosis, the Dunlaps were committed to bringing their little girl—whom they named Vivian—into the world and giving her the best life possible. They were not going to let the situation break them. In their minds, this was just an obstacle that was going to show their baby's character in a more definite way.

That's not to say that there weren't difficult moments; there were. There were times when Maria would get angry and fight with God. Rod had been crushed by Vivian's diagnosis and initially was unable to process any of it. That was his first experience with what he called "true, heartbreaking suffering." He'd never felt that way before. For Maria, it had meant that all of the hopes and dreams she'd had for her little girl had been dashed. This child, if she indeed survived, would have a very different kind of life from the one Maria had imagined for her.

Then something happened. There was a moment while Maria was pregnant that she felt God telling her this was all part of his will, that it would be for his glory and she didn't need to worry about it. That was the turning point in her heart. In her simple faith, she figured that if God had given her that message, then she would not worry. It took the pressure off anticipating what was going to happen to her child and stopped her from thinking about the worst-case scenario of what could happen. *God has this*, she kept telling herself. She had confidence that, regardless of what happened, God would use it for his glory.

"At that point, I truly believed Vivian was going to live," Maria said. "That was my hope and desire. Obviously, it wasn't God's. Still, I knew there was real purpose in everything that was happening."

Maria's younger sister was required to do a service project for her senior year of high school. Knowing that the weeks following the baby's birth could be taxing on Rod and Maria's time and finances, she decided to hold a walk to raise funds for their expenses. She called it "Vivian's Victory." In the months leading up to the walk, the weather had been sunny and dry. On the day of the walk, it rained in deluges, with one cloudburst after another. However, that did nothing to discourage walk participants. With each cloudburst, another large group of people arrived and joined in to support them. In hindsight, the Dunlaps see it as a foreshadowing of Vivian's life and the storm that they lived throughout it.

The week before Vivian was born, doctors met with Rod and Maria to discuss the complications and consequences that they might expect after the birth. They did not let the frightening details shake them. Instead, they prayed and waited. Vivian was born July 24, beautiful, pink, and screaming. Maria had been told that she wouldn't be able to hold her at all, but she was able to hold her briefly before she was whisked away to be hooked up to medical equipment to assist her. About an hour later, Rod and Maria baptized Vivian there in the hospital, and the journey began.

Shortly thereafter, it was determined that Vivian also had Turner syndrome, a rare genetic disorder affecting one in 2500 newborn girls. Although the specialists performed heart surgery on Vivian, the real problem was the rest of her internal anatomy, and specifically her lower intestines.

Vivian's Turner syndrome was severe, and she shouldn't even have survived the first trimester of the pregnancy. Her liver was on the other side of her body, she was missing her portal vein connecting her intestines to her liver, and she had a heart defect along with some other issues with her circulation. The doctors had never seen so many complications all together in one child. They didn't know how to move forward, but they decided to start with her heart and did the surgery. On August 1, Vivian had her first open heart surgery, and it turned out to be her only surgery. It became evident after a couple of days that she couldn't breathe but could do all the other bodily functions by herself. So she was repeatedly intubated and extubated. About a month into her life, the doctors concluded that Vivian needed a heart transplant. In fact, her heart was not the problem—it was working perfectly, and the blood was circulating correctly. The real problem was the anatomy of her body, specifically in her lower intestines and the way the veins were connected to everything else. Her veins were so narrow that there was too much pressure. Her body just couldn't do it.

On September 20, Vivian started throwing up blood. The medical team rushed into the room, and Maria was forced to make a sudden decision about what Vivian's plan would be.

"One of things that they always said to us was that you get to the point that you have to ask yourself if you are doing things for your child or for yourself," Maria told me. "That's the point we were at. We were doing things to her and nothing we were doing was helping her. We were just trying to make her get through it. I called Rod and told him that we had to make this decision. And so we decided to extubate her that night. The whole family came, and everybody got to see her. She stayed alive for quite a long time; she just kept hanging on. One of the really beautiful parts about that night was that Rod held her until she died. It was so beautiful for me because I brought her into the world, but my husband helped her as she was leaving it. So each had that moment. It was amazing."

Vivian's funeral was a few days later. The church was packed, including more than three hundred people Rod and

Maria had never met before. Maria had kept a blog throughout her pregnancy and while Vivian was alive, and because of that people all over the world came to know Vivian. The love that Vivian had brought with her into the world only multiplied after her death.

"People we didn't even know sent gift cards, gas cards, and other things right to the hospital to support us while we were there with her," Maria said. "We quickly realized we were the exception to the rule. We had all these people come be with us. They'd come be with me during the day and to watch her once a week so that Rod and I could go home. It was evident even before Vivian died that she brought so much love, joy, and goodness out of every person, even if she didn't meet them. Somehow, she touched their lives in some way. We knew that regardless of what happened to her, she had started something in our hearts, and we had to continue to help other people."

There was a good deal of money left from the Vivian's Victory walk, enabling the Dunlaps to pay off her funeral and medical costs. There still was money left, and they knew that they couldn't keep it because kind people had given it to them for Vivian. They'd heard stories of parents whose children were very sick or had been diagnosed with horrendous diseases and didn't have the money to care for them. Rod and Maria decided that they needed to help those families. This was the seed for the Vivian's Victory Foundation.[36]

The following year, the Dunlaps held another Vivian's Victory walk, and a multitude of people came. They contin-

---

36 Vivian's Victory, http://viviansvictory.org/.

ued to receive sizable donations and realized that they had to keep doing what they were doing—raising money to help other families in need. They continued doing the walk. They applied for nonprofit status and received it in 2014. The next year, they were able to assist over one hundred families. Next, they started an organization to help people with medical expenses or things that were specific to a specific disease. They consider it a blessing that they've been able to be a resource for these families, not only for financial needs, but also for support. Sometimes mothers call Maria just because they need someone to listen to them. She listens and offers them assurance and encouragement. What began as an event to raise money for their own expenses has become a beautiful ministry that has taken on a life of its own, and Vivian's Victory walk has become an annual event for the foundation.

"While I was pregnant, I dreamt about what our life would be like after Vivian was born, and then I realized that we'd never be able to do those things with her," Maria said. "Well, it's so awesome because I can do these things for other people. Vivian is a guiding force in everything we do. Because of her, all these families are going to benefit from what we're doing. This is the only gift that I get to give my daughter. It's overwhelming that she was fifty-nine days old when she died, and the impact that she's left on our world and that she continues to make is more than I will do in a hundred years. I was chosen to be her mom not just while she was alive, but even in her death. I'm the one who is chosen to bring hope to these families we serve. Our whole mission is to let these families know they're not alone. We want to touch as many people's lives as we can."

Maria remembers the first family that they were able to give money to. Their son had a very rare skin disease in which the skin just falls off. He had to be bandaged up multiple times a day. Rod worked with the boy's father, and one day he told Rod that insurance didn't cover the medication that his son needed to reduce the pain and protect him from complications. The medication cost $600 for a jar that lasted a week and a half. The Dunlaps gave the family the money they needed and were stirred by their gratitude.

"My daughter had so much purpose and has touched so many people," Maria said. "We had decided to name our baby Vivian, but only found out later that it meant "full of life." We knew then that there was something very special about this child."

When considering how God had worked in their lives through Vivian, Rod recalled that the first month after her death was one of the worst times in his life. He would swing back and forth between feeling normal and then finding himself crying and thinking about Vivian. He had never really grieved before, and he didn't know how to approach it. He was unhappy and confused about his faith. He knew that God loved them, but he had a hard time handling all the pain and suffering he was feeling.

Even though those months were difficult, Rod and Maria began to see more and more of what her brief life did in this world. They began receiving emails from people who had been brought closer to God by the Dunlap family's story or how Vivian's ability to be a fighter inspired them and made them wish they could be like her.

"It's pretty amazing to think back on it now—how a baby who can't even talk could change people's hearts," Rod said. "Only by the grace of God is this possible. Her suffering gave our suffering purpose. We could begin to see why everything happened, and it continues to become clearer and clearer. Because of her life, we now can help other families in need, just like others helped us. Her life has a purpose and still does. And because of that purpose, the hope that we received is not just for us. It's up to us to share that hope with others."

Surely, Rod and Maria would have preferred that Vivian had lived. Better yet, they would have preferred that she be born completely healthy and happy. They understood early on that their preferences were not part of God's omnipotent will. Eventually, they learned that God needed them for a special mission and that their daughter's life had a purpose beyond their comprehension. Yes, their path was accompanied by great sorrow. But in that sorrow, they discovered joy.

"There's no book, no step-by-step process to get from sorrow to joy," Maria said. "No one could tell you how to do that, and there's no timeline. But, it's there if you allow yourself to be open to it. The door of God's mercy and grace is always open. You just need to come through that open door."

The Dunlaps' story is one of shock, fear, trepidation, anguish, loss, grief, endurance, courage, hope, joy, and purpose. Regardless of the source of our sorrow, we can find a bit of ourselves in Rod and Maria Dunlap. Their sorrow was turned to joy in unexpected and humanly inexplicable ways. It's this that St. Thomas Aquinas refers to in this passage about the compassion of God:

> The more the heart of man is expanded by love of God and of his neighbor, and the more his meditations, his fervent prayers, his aspirations, his humility and his generosity have opened his soul to grace—the more elevated and greater is the grace that God the all-powerful will bestow upon him. And indeed, in the measure that a man seeks to conserve this grace and to use it for the praise of God and the common welfare, in the same measure will he receive a more abundant infusion of grace in this world and of glory in Paradise.[37]

When we're in the throes of turmoil, it may seem as though Jesus has hidden himself from us. But he assures us that, even though he isn't readily visible to us in our present crisis, it will last only a little while. Even when we can't see or feel him, he's there. The trials you endure now are much like those of a woman in labor, as our Lord tells us.

> "When a woman is in labor, she is in anguish because her hour has arrived; but when she has given birth to a child, she no longer remembers the pain because of her joy that a child has been born into the world." ✴ *John 16:21*

---

37 *The Ways of God for Meditation and Prayer*, by Saint Thomas Aquinas, 1995, Sophia Institute Press, p. 37-38.

The Dunlaps have proven that, even if the child brought into the world dies, she will have given new life to the world. The "child" you bring into the world through your suffering will give life to the world as well and you will no longer remember your anguish.

One day, our Lord will "reappear," bringing an end to your sorrow.

> "So you also are now in anguish. But I will see you again, and your hearts will rejoice, and no one will take your joy away from you." ✳ *John 16:22*

That is Jesus' promise.

Conclusion

GOD ALONE
IS MY JOY

J eremiah was known as the "weeping prophet" because
of his profound grief over the destruction of Jerusalem
by the Babylonians in 586 BC. He had warned the
Israelites that this would happen, and it did. Worse,
he had witnessed it with his own eyes without being able to
do a thing about it. These were his people! The ones he loved
and to whom he belonged. Jerusalem was the center of the
Israelites' world and the city that was home to the temple
King Solomon had built. He was beside himself.

Tradition holds that the prophet Jeremiah wrote
Lamentations—a book of beautiful poems and songs—
to express his sorrow. In the third chapter, he used three
symbols to represent his affliction: homelessness, wormwood, and gall.[38] St. John of the Cross explained the symbol-
ism and meaning of each in his *Ascent to Mount Carmel*.[39]

---

38 NRSVCE, Lamentations 3:19.

39 *Collected Works of St. John of the Cross*, trans. Kieran Kavanaugh, OCD,
    and Otilio Rodriguez, OCD, ICS Publications, 1979, p. 426.

Homelessness relates to the intellect and represents the riches of God's wisdom. Wormwood, a bitter herb, relates to the will. Gall, a poisonous plant by-product, relates to the memory, faculties, and strength. By using these three symbols, Jeremiah showed that Jerusalem's fall had deeply affected his ability to understand God's wisdom, accept his will, and stay strong in the face of this calamity and deal with the sad memories. These three sufferings mentioned by Jeremiah also relate to what is called the three theological virtues: faith, hope, and charity.

St. John of the Cross used the symbols of homelessness (intellect), wormwood (will), and gall (memory) as a means by which to explain true joy as that which can be found in God alone. Referring to the verse from Lamentations, the soul (Jeremiah) had no need to disclose his sufferings but instead had only to indicate his needs and let God do what he pleased.

"When the Blessed Virgin spoke to her beloved Son at the wedding feast in Cana in Galilee," St. John of the Cross wrote, "she did not ask directly for the wine, but merely remarked: *They have no wine* [Jn 2:3]. And the sisters of Lazarus did not send to ask our Lord to cure their brother, but to tell him that Lazarus whom he loved was sick [Jn 11:3]."

He gave three reasons for this. First, the Lord knows better than we do what is best for us. Second, God is more compassionate when he sees the needs and resignation of those who love and seek him. Third, indicating what we lack—our needs—rather than asking for what we, in our own opinion should have, safeguards us against self-love and possessiveness.

"The soul, now, does likewise by just indicating her three needs," he wrote. "Her words are similar to saying: Tell my Beloved, since I sicken and he alone is my health, to give me health; and, since I suffer and he alone is my joy, to give me joy; and, since I die and he alone is my life, to give me life."[40]

When you are in sorrow, the temptation is to tell God what you want him to do to alleviate your suffering. You tell him that he should take away this or give you back that. You might even get angry at him if he doesn't do as you wish. Or you might accuse him of being cruel. These are very human responses, and its okay to express them if you see them for what they are and don't let them take over your heart and mind or govern your actions or reactions. You are God's child and sometimes you need to sit at his feet and cry out to him. We all need that from time to time.

Afterwards, however, it's time to remember our Lord's promises and to again pledge your faithfulness to him. It's true that sorrow and joy aren't mutually exclusive and can take place at the same time. Because, even in the worst possible crisis, you can be sure that your sorrow will be turned to joy. That is Jesus' promise.

---

40 Ibid., p. 427.

ALSO AVAILABLE FROM
TWENTY-THIRD PUBLICATIONS

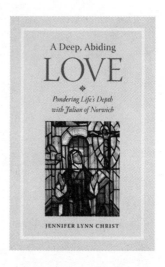

Holy Wind, Holy Fire

*Finding Your Vibrant Spirit
through Scripture*
PAMELA A. SMITH, SS.C.M.

The best way to experience the Spirit is to see what the Spirit does. In this beautiful book, Sr. Pamela invites us into a wonderful journey through the Old and New Testaments to catch glimpses of the Spirit at work. Reading, reflecting, and praying with this book will help to re-energize and reawaken us to the energy and joy that only the Holy Spirit can give.

136 PAGES | $14.95 | 5½" X 8½"
9781627853170

A Deep, Abiding Love

*Pondering Life's Depth
with Julian of Norwich*
JENNIFER LYNN CHRIST

Jennifer Christ draws parallels between Julian's times and ours and demonstrates how Julian's message of hope and joy in God's never-ending love for us can give us strength and hope. Spend time with this book—reading Julian's words, praying with them, pondering, and journaling, and letting her hope-filled message take root in your heart.

128 PAGES | $14.95 | 5½" X 8½"
9781627853156

TO ORDER CALL 1-800-321-0411
OR VISIT WWW.TWENTYTHIRDPUBLICATIONS.COM

TWENTY-THIRD PUBLICATIONS
A division of Bayard, Inc.